MW01256001

"How do you feel when someone says
away in horror, right? What about whe
interesting! Casey Hibbard is an exper
Stories That Sell will help you reach pe
storytelling."

David Meerman Scott,
Bestselling author of *The New Rules of Marketing and PR*

"People are often bored or put off by facts, but they never tire of hearing stories. That's
why selling with stories is so effective and that's why this book tells a crucial truth to
salespeople."

Jay Conrad Levinson, The Father of Guerrilla Marketing
Author, "Guerrilla Marketing" series of books

"In the age of The Jaded Customer, companies that can speak to prospects credibly and
authentically will thrive. In this timely, engaging and comprehensive book—and new
"standard" on the subject—case-study maven Casey Hibbard hasn't held back a single
how-to detail for turning satisfied customers' stories into a company's most powerful
selling tool. Perfect for both companies seeking a competitive edge in the marketplace
and writers looking to expand their professional offering."

Peter Bowerman, Author
The Well-Fed Writer titles
www.wellfedwriter.com

"A book-length tutorial on marketing with case studies and other customer success
stories has been long overdue. Casey Hibbard's *Stories That Sell* fills that gap admirably."

Bob Bly, Author, *The Copywriter's Handbook*, www.bly.com

"If your business sells costly or complex products or services, you must read this book.
Hibbard unveils the secrets to producing compelling success stories and case studies that
will grow your business. The chapter on securing permission from your best customers
contains a gold mine of ideas. This landmark book will become a standard reference guide
for businesses and writers."

Michael A. Stelzner,
Author of *Writing White Papers: How to Capture Readers and Keep Them Engaged*

"Using real customer scenarios with tangible business results is the best way to capture the
attention of busy decision makers. This fine book shows you how to craft these riveting
stories that move prospects to take action. Get it!"

Jill Konrath
Author, *Selling to Big Companies*
CEO, SellingtoBigCompanies.com

"Storytelling is the best way to attract prospects who increasingly rely on what they
hear to decide what they buy. Casey Hibbard has written an excellent, practical guide to
identifying and deploying powerful stories that will persuade and sell."

Lynn Upshaw (upshawmarketing.com),
Author of *Truth: The New Rules of Marketing in a Skeptical World*

Stories That Sell:
Turn Satisfied Customers into Your Most Powerful Sales & Marketing Asset

The Complete Guide to
Success-Story Marketing™

Casey Hibbard

Editor: Susan Mary Malone, Malone Editorial
Interior design and typesetting: Shawn Morningstar
Cover design: Joe Montgomery, Wednesday Design
Cover consulting: Susan Kendrick, Write to Your Market

Publisher's Cataloging in Publication
Hibbard, Casey

Stories that sell: turn satisfied customers into your most powerful sales & marketing asset/ Casey Hibbard

- 1st ed.
p. cm.

Includes index.

LCCN: 2008902180

ISBN-13: 978-0-615-18300-8

1.Marketing   2.Business Writing

658.8-dc22

For Scott, with love and gratitude

Table of Contents

CHAPTER SEVEN
STEP 5: CREATING COMPELLING STORIES 101

Acknowledgements

I extend heartfelt gratitude to all those who contributed to Stories That Sell and my path in getting here:

All the organizations and experts featured in this book: Each of you is a success story! Your willingness to share your knowledge and your own stories was essential to this project. It simply wouldn't be the same without these rich examples. Your creativity and best practices are an inspiration.

My clients: Thanks for allowing me the opportunity to tell your customer stories, and learn from you and your customers in the process.

Susan Mary Malone, Malone Editorial: It's easy to feel alone in this process. Your support and objective, big-picture feedback provided much-needed reassurance and peace of mind—and resulted in a better book.

Susan Kendrick, Write to Your Market (cover copy development): What a relief to put a head on this horseman! Your guidance and objective insight were invaluable.

Joe Montgomery, Wednesday Design: Talk about designs that sell! Your body of work sold me. What an enviable talent to turn abstract concepts into images that really communicate.

Ray Gulick, Evolution Web Development: Thanks for all your guidance in taking my online presence to the next level.

Peter Bowerman: You encouraged me to strive for a "seminal work" when I was so ready to be done with it already!

Michael Stelzner, WhitePaperSource: You're an inspiration and example of how to do it right! Thanks for answering my many questions.

Joseph Liberti of EQ at Work: Thanks for helping me realize that I need to tell stories.

My parents: For having the foresight somehow to name me Casey.

Dad: For always listening.

Mom: You saw my potential when I didn't, recognized the environments that would bring out my best, and showed me as much of the world as you possibly could. And I am forever grateful.

Scott: For all the brainstorming, pep talks, reality checks, and sanity checks. Thanks for enthusiastically encouraging my every dream and idea, being my partner in pursuit of them, and being a daily example of perseverance.

Casey Hibbard
November 2008

I

Introduction

"The fact is, everyone is in sales. Whatever area you work in, you do have clients and you do need to sell."

–Jay Abraham,
Getting Everything You Can out of All You've Got

In 2001, online relationship-service eHarmony.com was another dot-com at risk of becoming a dot-bomb. The company had burned through nearly all its initial venture-capital funding and struggled to stand out in a field of 3,000 online dating sites. Though unique among online dating services—with an emphasis on long-term relationships and a scientific method to successfully match people based on factors found to be present in enduring, happy marriages—eHarmony.com's message wasn't breaking through the noise. Now-famous founder Dr. Neil Clark Warren and then CEO Greg Forgatch considered closing while the company still had some cash to refund member subscriptions. "We were going to quit," Forgatch said. [1]

Then Warren appeared on James Dobson's radio show with ten successful eHarmony.com couples. It was a powerful combination: Dobson's wide audience, Warren's scientific approach, and the stories of real couples. "We got ninety thousand new referrals to our Web site, which overwhelmed any previous level of activity we had had," Warren said. [2] With a new infusion of cash, eHarmony.com began telling its success stories—with the voices of actual couples—in radio ads broadcast in a number of major American cities.

---

1. PBS, "Small Business School," 2003.
2. Buss, Dale. "Neil Warren: Online Passion." www.brandchannel.com, February 28, 2005.

From there, the company moved into television ads with the help of Santa Monica, California-based advertising firm Donat/Wald (www.donatwald.com). Again, those ads featured couples talking about their first phone conversations, first in-person meetings, what they love about each other, and how they got engaged—or even featured actual marriage proposals. While other online dating sites used photos of models or simple testimonials at the time, eHarmony.com began building trust, believability, and value in the eyes of potential members with true stories. "The campaign vividly showcases how eHarmony really does help people find their soul mates," said Lucas Donat, CEO, Donat/Wald. "The story of this brand is there, in the abundance of these heartfelt, compelling success stories." [3]

eHarmony.com quickly became the fastest growing net-based relationship service, now boasting 15,000 new members every day and an average of ninety marriages *every day*. The private company was expected to top $200 million in sales in 2007. [4] That growth is continuously fueled by word-of-mouth and heavy radio, TV, and online advertising. If you somehow have missed the company's ads, you can find them online, as well as learn about recent marriages or engagements, browse through written success stories, and peruse a section on eHarmony babies.

With every story told, eHarmony.com reinforces its brand and sets itself apart from the competition—goals of any business or organization.

Introducing Success-Story Marketing™

eHarmony.com is just one example of the power of Success-Story Marketing™, leveraging the stories of satisfied customers—in any form and any way—to communicate the benefits of products, services, causes, memberships, or ideas. *Stories That Sell* introduces Success-Story Marketing, detailing why it's so effective in promoting products, services, or organizations, and how to use it to grow your own business or cause.

---

3. "Donat/Wald Takes Wraps off New eHarmony 'Everlasting Love' Ad Campaign," Business Wire, March 1, 2005.

4. Parker, Emily. "The Matchmaker," The Wall Street Journal Online, February 10, 2007.

If it seems as though you're seeing more customer stories than ever, you are. And not just the age-old customer testimonial, but actual stories of how a product, service, or organization solved a problem. Pick up just about any magazine, turn on the TV, sort through your mail, or surf online and you'll see examples of organizations of every type telling the stories of their happiest, most-satisfied customers, members, or other beneficiaries. Increasingly, they are finding that true stories not only communicate credibility and results, but that those messages increase sales, shorten the sales cycle, help sell more to existing customers, land media coverage, and grow support for causes and ideas.

Jared Fogle, who lost more than 200 pounds by eating Subway® sandwiches every day, is not just Subway's poster child, but one of the most memorable examples of Success-Story Marketing. The OnStar service plays actual recordings from emergency calls. Visa customers talk about how the company smoothly and swiftly handled credit-card theft. Add to the list of Success-Story Marketers Microsoft, Geico, HP, Accenture, Pfizer, Dell, Dow Chemical, IBM, Verizon, The Humane Society of the United States, and Ford Motor Corporation.

Although not a new concept, it has reached new levels in recent years. These days, so much competition exists, so much media noise, and unfortunately, too many companies that have been less than trustworthy or closed overnight that we need more evidence to make buying decisions. Just as reality-TV caters to a public craving real stories, Success-Story Marketing fills a need for buyers to understand the experiences of other buyers. Consider Amazon.com, where customers make purchase decisions based on reviews submitted by other buyers.

The global, online nature of business also changes marketing communications. Not all that long ago, we conducted business mostly face to face. The first impression a potential customer had of a business was from an in-person experience with its people. Customers could see smiling faces or family photos on the desk, and began to build trust. With the breadth and reach of communications now, buyers are no longer limited to buying car insurance from their friendly neighborhood agent, but also have an assortment of national car-insurance companies from which to choose. At once, we have more choices than ever before, and often without the advantage of a face-to-face or even voice-to-voice connection to ease the decision-making process.

We're given email, online chat, or instant messaging—instead of a live person—with which to get our questions answered before making a purchase.

Customer stories serve a role that no other promotional tools truly fill by accomplishing three key purposes at once: credibility, education, and validation. Brochures, Web content, and data sheets tout the company line, in the company's own language, and though they may educate readers, they don't carry as much credibility as the customer's word. Likewise, those pieces often leave readers wondering how a product or service actually works in a real setting. Testimonials bolster a company's credibility, but don't educate audiences or validate solutions very thoroughly. White papers, while sometimes including customer stories, are largely educational and too thorough for many audiences and certain parts of the sales process. Many just want an overview of the customer's experience. Customer stories complement all other communications and bridge a gap between an organization and its prospects.

As in school classrooms, entertainment, and social bonding, it's the act of storytelling that keeps audiences interested, engaged, and able to remember information.

For nearly a decade, I have specialized in creating customer stories for organizations, not just writing them, but helping companies put in place and refine their Success-Story Marketing processes and practices. After time as a marketing copywriter for the University of California, Davis, and a high-tech reporter for a city business journal, I went out as a freelance marketing-communications writer. Whatever the subject matter, I was always looking for the most compelling way to tell true stories.

Focusing on customer stories led me to form Compelling Cases, Inc., to provide specialized customer-story development and coordination for organizations. Now, with more than 450 customer stories behind me, I wrote *Stories That Sell* to bring together all the best practices and tips I've picked up over the years, as well as those of a number of organizations large and small. It's effectively a book of success stories about using customer stories.

Stories That Sell provides a roadmap for how to plan stories strategically, gather the best information from customers, create compelling stories, use stories throughout your sales, marketing, and public-relations efforts—and interface collaboratively with customers. Much more than just capturing customers' experiences, Success-Story Marketing requires that you partner with your most satisfied customers to create something that's win-win for vendor and customer alike.

A Proven Process

The Seven-Step Customer-Story System, highlighted in chapters two through nine, provides a defined process—in place at best-practices organizations today—to ensure you create the customer stories that are most effective for your organization, manage a smooth flow with customers and internal stakeholders, and get maximum mileage out of your stories. Whether you're a marketing manager tasked with starting a new customer-story program, a business owner wanting to set yourself apart from the competition, or a writer looking to create stories, you'll benefit from understanding what works and what doesn't throughout the process.

A Focus on Written Stories

Stories That Sell focuses primarily on written stories (even though audio/visual formats can be valuable additions to your marketing mix). When you create written customer stories, you document a customer's experience in a way that can be used again and again—on your Web site, in press releases, in PowerPoint presentations, in white papers, in articles, in newsletters, for awards submissions, and so on. Marketing today is very content driven. Search-engine optimization requires rich Web site content. When prospects are searching online for a product or service like yours, you need all the content you can get to help increase your search-engine relevance.

Business-to-Business Emphasis

Nearly any organization can use its customer stories to grow a business, idea, or cause. *Stories That Sell* includes examples from all types and sizes of for-profit and nonprofit organizations. However, a majority of examples in this book are from business-to-business (B2B) companies (primarily because more B2B companies create customer stories than do organizations selling to consumers). There are simply more examples out there in B2B. Yet, the featured companies employ best practices from which just about everyone can learn and then apply in their own way, in their own environments.

Definitions

A lot of confusion exists about what to call customer stories. Refer to the Don't-Miss Definitions section for names and definitions related to Success-Story Marketing. However, throughout the book, *Stories That Sell* generally refers to any type of story featuring customer successes as "customer stories."

How to Use This Book

Stories That Sell is designed to be a resource for anyone who manages or creates customer stories. The information draws on ten years of day-to-day work with customer stories, along with the experiences of dozens of companies. Some parts will be applicable to you now, while others might be down the road. The book provides a framework on which to build your customer-story program, and expand it as you go. Implement some ideas now, and add more later.

Read the complete book first, as each chapter adds to the one before and takes you through the complete Seven-Step Customer-Story System. Then keep it handy as a reference when issues or challenges arise, or if you're looking for new ideas to enhance your existing program. The table of contents is organized to help you quickly locate answers to the issue of the day. Also, find other resources, customer stories, and learning opportunities online at www.StoriesThatSellGuide.com.

If you're a writer, you will be most interested in chapters seven and eight, Intelligence Gathering and Creating Compelling Stories. However, many times arise when knowledge of the complete process covered in the book will be valuable to you and all the parties you are working with.

The last sub-heading of the Leveraging Customer Stories chapter addresses ways that nonprofits or causes can use their stories to further their organizations. However, nonprofits can learn from all the other chapters, just as for-profit organizations can pick up tips from the featured organizations in the nonprofit section.

Hopefully, you will take away dozens of ideas for leveraging stories on satisfied customers to build trust with your audiences, shorten the sales cycle, sell more to existing customers, win PR, land investors, and ultimately grow your organization.

Keep up with conversation and best practices related to customer stories with the free *Stories That Sell* e-Tip of the Month and the *Stories That Sell* Blog. Both are available at www.StoriesThatSellGuide.com.

Don't-Miss Definitions

Before moving ahead, familiarize yourself with some of the terms you'll see throughout the book.

Success-Story Marketing™

Stories That Sell introduces Success-Story Marketing as the term to describe the act of leveraging the stories of satisfied customers—in any form and any way—for promotional purposes. Dozens of ways are available to market your products or services by using your customers' stories. When you see this term, it simply refers to the entire genre of customer-story use.

Types of Customer Stories

Customer stories go by a number of different names: case studies, success stories, case histories, case examples, customer/member profiles, and user stories, just to name a few. Your organization may have its own favorite name for them. They all basically refer to the same thing —featuring a customer's or beneficiary's experience with a product, service, or organization. In the interest of clarifying the nomenclature for customer stories (and being on the same page throughout the book), let's define the types of customer stories.

This book often talks about the use of stories *in general*. When not referring to a particular type, *Stories That Sell* simply uses the term "customer stories."

Success Story

Stories That Sell defines two types of customer stories: *success stories* and *case studies*. Most customer stories are basically success stories. A success story is effectively an overview of the customer's experience with your products, services, or company. It usually covers who the customer is, why the company or person needed your solution, how she picked you as her vendor, the customer's experience of the solution, the benefits, and results. The story covers each of these areas, but does not go into *extensive* detail on any topics.

Depending on your audience, success stories can be as short as a paragraph or two, or up to two or three pages. Success stories work most effectively with audiences who want that complete overview, such as executive-level decision-makers. However, for some readers, they may not provide enough detail to make a purchase decision.

Case Study

Case studies, usually two or more pages, go into more specifics about one or more customers, providing greater detail about certain aspects of a customer's experience. Instead of an overview in a success story, a case study often goes more in-depth regarding parts of the customer's experience. Some audiences, such as those in technical roles, want and need this additional detail to assist with decision-making. They need to see specifically how a solution works in a similar customer's environment, not just for increased confidence in the purchase, but also to educate themselves on successful practices of other companies. Many managers also like the additional detail that a case study provides, but they usually prefer business benefits and results rather than "how it works" information.

These are just some generalizations. Chapter Seven, Creating Compelling Stories, covers customer-story types in greater depth.

Testimonials

What about the age-old testimonial? Blurbs of glowing praise from customers, usually one to several sentences, do have a place in establishing credibility in buyers' minds. They fit nicely as highlights on your Web site, or in brochures and datasheets. But they can't educate and validate your solutions the way detailed stories can. By all means, continue to use testimonials, and even pull customer quotes out of your customer stories. But only stories can accomplish, at once, credibility, education, and validation. More on that in Chapter Two.

References

Similar to references when you're job-hunting, a "reference" is a customer willing to endorse or "vouch for" your company, product, or service.

Organizations approach their satisfied customers about being "reference customers." As such, reference customers participate in a number of possible activities: being featured in a customer story, talking one-on-one with prospects, speaking at events, writing articles, or talking to the media, for example.

Customer-Reference Programs

Many companies have customer-reference programs, which provide a more formal way to encourage, qualify, and track customers who are willing to serve as references in some capacity. Customer stories are just one product of a customer-reference program.

If needed, refer back to this section as you encounter these terms in context throughout the book.

1

The Power of
Success-Story Marketing™

"If you tell me, it's an essay. If you show me, it's a story."

—Barbara Greene, children's author

Whether we're aware of it or not, as humans, we tend to follow certain patterns of trust and decision-making. Success-Story Marketing—using customer, beneficiary, or member stories to advance a product, service, idea, or cause—caters to some of the fundamentals of human behavior:

- We trust what others say much more than what a business itself says

- We look to others to determine how we should act

- We love to hear about other people

In Friends and Strangers We Trust

Think back to the last time you tried a new restaurant or watched a movie. How did you choose where to eat or what to see? You probably saw newspaper advertisements, and maybe even interviews with stars of the show. But chances are, you really picked the place or the movie on the recommendation of a friend, family member, or coworker. If not one of those, then it was likely due to a good review in the newspaper or online from people you trust as authorities on cuisine or cinema.

And what about your latest electronics or vehicle purchase? Maybe you talked with others who have brands and models you're considering, consulted *Consumer Reports* for ratings, or checked online sites with customer reviews. Likewise, you probably wouldn't select a realtor, babysitter, financial advisor, or any other important service provider without some sort of positive third-party endorsement.

In fact, information put out by actual companies ranks low on the list of trusted sources as buyers make decisions. The business itself is good for details such as specifications, how something works, or pricing. But most of us don't truly believe the benefits espoused by companies–unless they are verified by other trusted sources. Just about everyone else is more credible than the business itself.

The following survey by Bridge Ratings and the University of Massachusetts, published on eMarketer.com, breaks down trusted sources of information.

Trusted Sources of Information according to US Consumers, 1997 & 2007 (rated on a scale of 1-10)

	1997 University of Massachusetts survey	2007 Bridge Ratings survey
Friends, family and acquaintances	8.8	8.6
Strangers with experience	4.2	7.9
Teachers	9.2	7.3
Religious leaders	9.0	6.9
Newspapers and magazines	8.1	6.1
Favorite radio personality	6.8	5.5
TV news reporters	7.5	5.2
Bloggers	*	2.8
Advertising	3.3	2.2
Telemarketers	2.1	1.8

Note: 2007 n=3,400 ages 13+; in both surveys, respondents were asked this question, "Please rate on a scale of 1 to 10 the following as sources of information you most trust"; *not asked in the 1997 survey
Source: Bridge Ratings and the University of Massachusetts as cited in press release, August 1, 2007

086253   www.eMarketer.com

On a scale of 1-10, "Strangers with experience" receives
a 7.9 in a survey of trusted sources of information,
while a company's own advertising receives a 2.2.

As expected, someone you know personally tops the list, with "strangers with experience" a close second, and the media falling in behind. Comparatively, advertising (vendor-produced promotional materials) scored a two-point-two on a scale of one to ten. Advertising has its place in creating awareness, but clearly must be backed up by other sources to get buyers to make a purchase. Customer stories perfectly fill the "strangers with experience" category, providing the third-party validation that buyers, donors, or others need to make a decision about products, services, or an organization.

The 'Like Me' Factor

As teenagers, we begin rebelling and expressing our individuality–by looking and dressing *just like* all our friends or the celebrities we admire. According to Robert B. Cialdini, author of *Influence: The Psychology of Persuasion,* that's because the actions of others help us decide how we ourselves should act. He calls it "social proof," or the "like me" factor. "The principle of social proof operates most powerfully when we are observing the behavior of people just like us. That is why I believe we are seeing an increasing number of average-person-on-the-street testimonials on TV these days... As a rule, we make fewer mistakes by acting in accordance with social evidence than contrary to it."[5] People perceive less risk when others have successfully gone before them.

James March and Johan Olsen named a similar concept the "logic of appropriateness." They say decisionmaking results from following a set of rules consistent with an identity.[6] In other words, people ask themselves, "What would someone like me or an organization like this do in this situation?" If it's our nature to emulate others, especially people or organizations we admire, then customer stories provide a model of behavior for audiences–even more so if the featured customer has faced similar challenges or is in the same industry as the reader. In fact, the more the story sounds like the prospective customer's situation, the more relevant and valuable it is in the decision-making process.

5. Cialdini, Robert B., *Influence: The Psychology of Persuasion.*
6. Marsh, James G. & Olsen, Johan P., *The Institutional Dynamics of International Political Orders.*

We Love to Hear about Other People

People are also people oriented. On a personal level, we want to know what our neighbors are up to, or our favorite celebrities. Human-interest stories in the media are always the most captivating. The same goes in business. Even when you're talking about products and services, readers are more engaged when there's a human element. Products and services don't function on their own; rather, people interact with them. People encounter challenges to overcome, become heroes, find solutions, and ultimately triumph. Following the basic journalism rule, "people love to read about people," customer stories provide the perfect framework to capture the human elements of just about any situation.

Stories Make it Stick

Stories play a starring role as one of the "six principles of sticky ideas" in Chip Heath and Dan Heath's popular book, *Made to Stick*. Sticky ideas or concepts leave an impression on audiences, helping them remember and understand. The Heaths assert that stories provide both simulation (the opportunity to imagine scenarios), and inspiration (which comes from seeing others' successes and being moved to act as a result). At the same time, stories provide the opportunity to integrate three other *Made to Stick* principles of sticky messaging:

Concreteness—A way of making abstract concepts more concrete and understandable, such as how technology works.

Credibility—The opportunity to provide a level of detail, which is more convincing than a lack of specifics.

Emotion—Again, providing specifics gets people emotionally engaged in a way that generalizations do not.

Stories help people imagine scenarios and gain inspiration from seeing others' successes—and they are moved to act as a result.

The 3 Roles of Success-Story Marketing

With the science of stories behind us, let's talk about the practical aspects of using customer stories to help persuade audiences to buy a product, try a service, or support a nonprofit:

- Credibility
- Education
- Validation

Credibility: A Real Company with Real Customers

As the graph on trusted information sources indicates (see page 12), it's hard to establish credibility in buyers' minds without third-party evidence. Otherwise, they find it too much of a leap of faith. And the need for evidence is directly proportional to the price tag, perceived level of risk involved, and importance of the decision to the buyer or company. We don't need nearly as much information or validation to make a decision about which ice cream to try as we do about which car to buy.

In recent years, the need for credibility has only accelerated. In the '90s and 2000s, the business world saw a number of shake-ups that have left buyers understandably leery about the companies to do business with. In the early part of the new millennium, quite a few major companies were discovered to have unethical or illegal business practices. Enron was the most high profile of the bunch, with irregular accounting procedures bringing the company to bankruptcy in 2001. Its accounting firm, the once prestigious Arthur Andersen, fell soon after. And then came Tyco and WorldCom.

About the same time, the high-tech bubble burst after many heady years, resulting in countless corporate casualties. Companies were open one day and closed the next. They would spend years developing a product, with no income, until finally they had to close their doors. Venture-capital firms and banks couldn't keep throwing money at businesses taking too long to reach a profit.

After all that, buyers are understandably hesitant about the products and services they choose. Will the company be around next month to create new-product releases and provide adequate product support?

"The need for documented customer successes has been largely driven by the technology sector," says Steven Nicks, Partner and Co-founder of Phelon Group (www.phelongroup.com), a firm that focuses on customer retention, referability, and repurchase. "In the late '90s, we saw people making major technology purchases that didn't pan out, so in subsequent years people demanded to hear from those individuals who had already successfully deployed the solution. And for the savvy tech company, it was a way of gaining credibility and a competitive edge."

While having real customer stories doesn't ensure a business won't go under, it does demonstrate that an organization has actual customers using products and services–and seeing results. That goes a long way toward establishing peace of mind for audiences.

Education: Show, Don't Tell

Marketers and business owners put a lot of thought into how they communicate about their offerings. But as much as they detail how their products and services work for users, there's often a gap between those descriptions and readers' understanding of how they will actually work in their environments–all the more so when the products or services are complex. Remember the lesson from high school English class, "Show, don't tell?" You have to show readers what you're talking about, descriptively and in context, rather than just telling them that your product or service accomplishes this or that. Mark Twain put it another way, "Don't say the old lady screamed—bring her on and let her scream."

Buyers have a lot of questions. How will services be delivered in our environment? How is this vendor different from others? How long does an implementation take and who's involved? How will a product generate time-savings in our workflow? What can we expect in terms of ongoing support? What does the vendor do that gets the results we want?

Customer stories answer many of their questions. They are especially effective when they mirror the reader's situation. A growing manufacturing company wants to hear how another similar manufacturing company reduced production time. A small business needs to understand how a search-engine optimization firm increased Web site traffic for a similar business. Customer stories offer the perfect opportunity to show a product or service in action for a customer, making them very valuable marketing and sales tools. It's just the type of information buyers are looking for as they learn about a solution or organization.

A survey by KnowledgeStorm (www.knowledgestorm.com) and MarketingSherpa (www.marketingsherpa.com) sheds light on the role of case studies, particularly in IT purchase decisions. The survey, with results published in *How Technology Marketers Meet Buyers' Appetite for Content*, asked nearly 4,000 B2B marketers, and technology and business professionals, what buyers want and what marketers deliver. The survey revealed that buyers expect you to educate them. In fact, eight-four percent said they want content that educates them and expect vendors to provide it. [7]

Customer stories provide critical education about how solutions actually work in real environments.

Guerrilla Marketing for Consultants, by Jay Conrad Levinson and Michael W. McLaughlin, stresses the importance of customer stories in helping prospects understand exactly what it would be like to work with a consultant. "These documents can answer the number one question clients ask consultants: 'How will your team work with our team to achieve the results we need?' Case studies also clarify approaches, strategies, and resources that you have successfully employed on other projects." [8]

Validation: Demonstrating Results

Everyone has competition, whether it's another organization like yours or the current arrangement in prospective customers' environments. In *Selling to Big Companies*, author Jill Konrath points out that the status quo is often your biggest competition. Even if companies have problems to resolve and opportunities for improvement, they "just have so much on their plate that they can't add one more thing–no

---

7. KnowledgeStorm and MarketingSherpa, *How Technology Marketers Meet Buyers' Appetite for Content*.
8. Levinson, Jay Conrad and McLaughlin, Michael W., *Guerrilla Marketing for Consultants*.

matter how worthwhile it seems." [9] Therefore, you have to demonstrate that the short-term pain of making a change is worthwhile in the long run.

Likewise, with so many options out there, buyers are cynical and believe another solution just like yours is around the corner, maybe even at a lower price. "The only thing that seems to counteract it is real customer stories with actual, tangible, and measurable results," Konrath says.

Boosting Buyer Confidence

Customer stories provide that critical validation that gets prospects' attention at multiple points in the sales cycle. Seeing clear results at other organizations like theirs helps buyers more easily make the decision to purchase, and eliminates risk in their minds. That doesn't mean that you shouldn't create detailed brochures and Web sites. They certainly provide important information for decision-makers. But for ultimate impact, you have to back them with real customer stories, results, and quotes.

Findings on Customer-Story Effectiveness

Customer stories and anecdotes are powerful for just about any type of organization. But because they have typically been more a marketing staple of high-tech companies, the small amount of research available tends to be related to technology purchases. The survey, *How Technology Marketers Meet Buyers' Appetite for Content* [10], revealed intriguing findings on the role of customer stories:

- Sixty-seven percent of those surveyed often read case studies (customer stories) in the buying decision–putting case studies as the #2 choice just behind white papers in terms of desired content.

---

9. Konrath, Jill, *Selling to Big Companies*.
10. KnowledgeStorm and MarketingSherpa, *How Technology Marketers Meet Buyers' Appetite for Content*.

- **Buyers like objectivity**–Customer stories, articles from industry journalists, and analyst reports are all frequently forwarded by buyers. The study indicates the perception of objectivity makes them of interest to the broadest number of individuals in the IT decision process.

- **Buyers need to solve a problem**–When they start the search for a new technology, nearly seventy-two percent of respondents want to find "solutions to solve a current problem." Customer examples show very clearly *how* a solution solves a specific problem.

- **They want it targeted for them!**–Nearly eighty-two percent of technology buyers prefer information targeted to their industry. Customer stories are a key way to demonstrate real-world successes with specific industries and types of problems.

Similarly, when TechTarget (www.techtarget.com) and CMO Council (www.cmocouncil.org) took a closer look at the inner workings of how information technology (IT) buyers make purchasing decisions in its *2007 Technology Buying and Media Consumption Benchmarking Survey*, they found an interesting gap between case-study use and effectiveness. Twenty-eight percent of IT buyers surveyed use customer case studies in technology purchases. But when used, they had a *seventy-five percent rate of effectiveness*. The survey pointed out that customer stories showed the greatest gap between effectiveness and actual use of all the marketing communications it asked about. That led the survey writers to predict that they are poised for increased use in the future.

Minimize Live Reference Calls

It's clear that third-party validation is critical. Many businesses turn to their best customers to serve as live references on calls with prospects. Yet, there's only so often you can call on busy current customers to participate in these activities, and they may not be available right when you need them. When you create a written customer story, you document the details of that customer's experience once, and then that story often replaces a live reference call. In fact, by reducing reference calls, you can look at customer stories as effective relationship management with your most valued customers.

KnowTia, maker of OasisCRM software (www.oasiscrm.com), saw a significant drop in the need for live reference calls when it began documenting its customer stories. Before, the company regularly arranged calls between prospects and current customers. "In the first year of using success stories, we only had one live reference call," said Jeffrey White, Vice President of Sales. "Those stories give prospects the detail they need to understand other customers' experiences without having to talk to an actual current customer."

By capturing stories of customers that are just like your prospects, those "strangers with experience" serve as compelling examples to your audience, giving them the confidence to buy from or back your organization.

Chapter Take-Aways

- We trust what other people say about products and services more than what a business itself says.

- People look to others like themselves to determine how they should act.

- Even when you're talking about products and services, readers are more engaged when there's a human element involved.

- Stories make concepts and ideas memorable, understandable, concrete, and emotionally engaging.

- Stories accomplish three key objectives for readers: credibility, education, and validation.

- Testimonials serve mainly to establish credibility.

- Technology buyers prefer information targeted to their industry. Customer stories are a key way to demonstrate real-world successes with specific industries and types of problems.

- Customer stories minimize the need for live customer-reference calls.

2

The Seven-Step Customer-Story System

"You have to understand, my dears, that the shortest distance between truth and a human being is a story."

—Anthony de Mello, *One Minute Wisdom*

The end goal is simple: a completed, approved customer story, ready for use. Yet, the path to get there involves multiple steps, companies, and individuals. From start to finish, you're collaborating with internal parties and your most satisfied customers, making it essential to have a smooth-running process that respects customers' time and their willingness to share their information publicly.

This chapter introduces the time-tested Seven-Step Customer-Story System, the complete process of executing Success-Story Marketing. Through managing hundreds of customer stories over the years, I established this process and find it to be the most effective approach for organizations and their featured customers. It ensures everyone involved in the process knows what to expect and what comes next, making for a much smoother experience for all. Whether you already have a process in place or are starting a customer-story program from scratch, you'll learn how to enhance the process and how to trouble-shoot challenges that arise.

Here's an overview of the seven steps. Subsequent chapters delve deeper into the details of each step.

Step 1: Strategic Story Planning (Chapter Three)

For many companies, customer stories are high on the marketing wish list. However, finding willing and able customer candidates can be a challenge. That constant need for more stories, coupled with the challenges of finding them, often leads to a "take-anything" attitude. Quantity wins out over quality when trying to meet targets.

Strategic story planning ensures that you create the stories stakeholders need, and those stories accomplish their goals. Like any marketing initiative, it's critical to tie customer stories to your current objectives. That means assessing your current inventory, regularly communicating with those who use stories to understand their needs, learning from satisfied customers how and why they made buying decisions, and creating an actionable "wish list" of stories to pursue. Finally, you have to communicate your needs to all, often.

Step 2: Uncovering Customer Candidates (Chapter Four)

Most likely, incredible stories exist among your customer base. But how do you find the strongest ones? Drawing story leads from protective sales representatives and partners/resellers requires creativity, relationship-building, and continuous communication regarding the types of stories you need. But the payoff is a steady stream of customer candidates to pursue.

Step 3: Securing Customer Permission (Chapter Five)

Though your customers may be exceptionally happy, securing permission to feature them by name is not always easy—especially when big names are involved. Some may readily agree while others require more discussion and negotiation. Companies that succeed do their homework to understand customers' goals and challenges, talk openly with customers about what they are willing and able to participate in, and then create win-win proposals that, at once, meet their own needs as well as customers' objectives.

Step 4: Intelligence Gathering (Chapter Six)

A story is only as strong as the information you have to create it. Effective information-gathering requires a solid understanding of the solutions to be featured and the most important value propositions to include, and then as much background information as possible before actually interviewing customers. It's also critical to talk with the right customer contacts to ensure the end story resonates with readers. Interview questions must draw out the details you need and help customers provide measurable results. Finally, the process should be as quick, simple, and painless for customers as possible.

Step 5: Creating Compelling Stories (Chapter Seven)

In the realm of customer stories, "compelling" means merging what readers want to know with what you want them to know—and then tying all that up in a format that is attractive and readable. The format, length, and type of story completely depend on your audience. Every story should be designed to cater to both skimmers and those who read the complete text, making powerful headlines, subheads, and call-out information critical.

Step 6: Story Signoff (Chapter Eight)

It's not over until the customer signs on the dotted line, or at least gives you some sort of documented permission to use the story. The review process includes internal contacts, partners, and customers, and sometimes involves some friendly negotiation to ensure the story meets the objectives of all those parties. Internal and external reviewers are all busy people—and your story may not be at the top of their list—so employ polite persistence until you secure permission. When it's all over, always remember to thank your customers formally for their time and participation.

Step 7: Leveraging Customer Stories (Chapter Nine)

A story highlighting a customer's success with products or services is one of the most versatile types of promotional content any organization can create. There are a number of different ways and places where you can use a story to establish or reinforce credibility, educate audiences, and validate products and services:

Building a Brand
- Advertising
- Campaigns

Marketing Communications
- Web sites
- Online customer communities
- Other online opportunities
- Newsletters
- Events
- Direct marketing

Selling with Stories
- Training new sales reps
- Examples in PowerPoint presentations
- Sales letters
- Email
- Voice mail
- Sales conversations
- Proposals
- Case-study booklets
- Up-selling, cross-selling with existing accounts
- An alternative to live reference calls
- Venture-capital proposals/presentations

Spinning Success Stories into Media Coverage
- Press releases
- Pitching stories to the media
- Contributed articles
- Industry awards submissions

Telling Tales to Further Causes

- Employee/volunteer orientation
- Web site
- Fundraising appeals
- Grant proposals
- Newsletters/magazines
- Annual reports
- Advertising/public-service announcements
- Speeches and meetings
- Your physical environment
- Your hold message
- Public relations

A defined process keeps all parties on the same page and helps you maximize your investment in customer stories. From start-to-finish, stories are planned, created, and used with an end goal in mind.

3

Step 1:
Strategic Story Planning

"Storytelling is the most powerful way to put ideas into the world today."

-Robert McKee, *Story Structure Workshop*

S trategic story planning is the first step in the Seven-Step Customer-Story System. Planning helps ensure that the stories you pursue and create truly do support your objectives. Companies spend untold time and energy rounding up customer candidates, convincing customers to go on record, creating stories, and getting them approved for use. After all that, many stories are never used to their full potential.

"We discovered that the majority of customer content developed today is not powerful and, in most cases, is not used effectively, if at all," says Steven Nicks, Partner and Co-founder of Phelon Group (www.phelongroup.com). The firm, which focuses on customer retention, referability, and repurchase, has worked with senior sales and marketing executives at a number of enterprise companies. According to Phelon Group, the problem stems from not matching story development with actual company needs.[11]

---

11. *Success Sells*, Phelon Consulting Services, 2004.

Why do companies that meticulously plan all their marketing-communications activities, tying them to current initiatives and key messages, lack this conscientious approach when it comes to story development? Too often, they focus on quantity—meeting numbers promised to the sales force—rather than quality. Teams are tasked with producing a certain number of stories, which can lead to a take-anything attitude—especially considering the difficulty of getting customers to go on record. Take anyone who says yes!

I see this frequently in working with companies on customer stories. A sales or account rep, or an external partner/reseller, will recommend a candidate for a customer story. The company often agrees to move ahead even if it already has sufficient customer stories for that particular niche of products/services, industry, and geography. If the sales force already has stories that fit this niche, they likely don't need more. It's probably not a wise use of budget funds to capture story types that are already represented in your database, unless it's a new or updated version of the product, the customer has a particularly unique story or quantifiable benefits, or the company needs more stories for PR efforts.

Don't pursue a customer story just because a happy customer is willing and able; make sure the story truly fills a niche in your sales, marketing, and PR plans.

Realizing that just any story doesn't necessarily meet their needs, many are beginning to focus on quality. "Historically, marketing has been out there creating stories based on opportunistic examples that present themselves instead of creating stories based on where sales is headed and what projected future needs are," Nicks says. "We see the trend moving away from volume and people investing their content budget in a way that aligns more with the needs of the sales force. Now it's much more aligned with, 'Does the story really fit our needs?' and 'How does this story move the prospect to the next phase of the sales cycle?'"

Of course, start-up companies or organizations just beginning to create stories are an exception. In the early days when customers are few and far between, early-stage businesses take just about any story possible to begin building their credibility as real companies with real customers. But it's still important to ensure that every story communicates the right messages and serves a purpose in sales, marketing, and PR. As the company grows, it can be more discriminating in story selection.

Story Needs-Assessment

Story Inventory

Strategic story planning starts with a needs assessment, performed thoroughly and regularly. Those who manage stories at an organization should first inventory the current stories that are available. Look at each and note which categories and "themes" it hits:

- Products/services
- Industry
- Customer size
- Geography
- Business problem addressed with solutions
- Focus: either technical detail or business case
- Other themes that matter to your company, such as product flexibility, tech support, assistance from a consulting-services team, etc.

These will vary from company to company, so determine which ones are relevant to your business. Create a spreadsheet that lists all current customer stories, and their associated categories and themes. The following is just a basic example:

Story Inventory Matrix

	Flagship product	Module A	Module B	Professional services	Small to mid-size	Enterprise
Customer Story A	X	X		X		X
Customer Story B	X		X		X	

Inventory your current databank of customer stories across all areas relevant to your organization to find gaps. Keep this matrix up to date as the story inventory changes. Also keep track of each story's age and all the ways your company has used it.

The Story Wish List

With a full inventory of all the customer stories you currently have, assess which additional stories the organization still needs to meet its objectives.

Consult Stakeholders

Talk with all parties that rely on customer stories, including sales reps, account reps, partners/resellers, marketing, and PR representatives. Make notes about what works now and needs improvement:

- How do they currently use stories—with which audiences in which part of the cycle?
- Do they find that stories in their current forms are valuable for the ways and times they need to leverage them?
- Are they able to locate the right story quickly for an opportunity?
- What is missing from the current inventory that would help with their efforts?
- Do certain themes or angles need to be included in future stories?
- Do they have any specific events coming up where they need certain materials, such as industry-specific trade shows, product launches, or PR opportunities?
- Can they recommend any good candidates to be customer references or stories?

Health care	Gov.	Manu.	Addresses compliance	Operational efficiency	North/South America	Asia-Pacific
X				X	X	
		X	X		X	

Phelon Group also recommends asking current customers who in their organizations helped make the buying decisions and what factors influenced them, and then creating stories that model those successful outcomes. "Learn what makes them tick and leverage that learning across similar prospects."[12]

Rather than talking with all these folks ad hoc, meet with representatives of each group once or twice a year, or survey the field regularly. A large data-storage-solutions company, discussed later in the "Selling with Stories" sub-chapter, surveyed its sales reps online to determine how current stories met their needs and what sales reps required to sell more effectively. The insights were extremely valuable in helping the company plan future stories.

Also, check in with these parties as any major changes occur with the company or industry that may affect story needs, such as new products/services, new marketing campaigns, new industry regulations, or new competition. Finally, encourage regular, open dialogue between those using and those creating stories, regarding how effective stories are and what the field still needs.

With a clear idea of what you need to round out your inventory, compare that against your budget and create an actionable "wish list" of projects to pursue. The wish list may look similar to the matrix of your existing stories. Which products/services, industries, geographies, company sizes, and other themes do you need to fulfill the wish list?

---

12. *Success Sells*, Phelon Consulting Services, 2004.

A single story typically hits multiple categories. To maximize the budget, some companies try to pack in as many products and services as possible into a single story. That might be valuable if you're trying to show that all your products and services work together to get the desired end result. But otherwise, including lots of products or themes in a single story may be too general and unfocused for your audience. Taking a more narrow focus allows you to provide more details about a few solutions.

Also, create a plan for how you will use each story. For example, Customer A's story will be part of a new product launch on X date, a media pitch to a trade magazine on X date, highlighted in the newsletter, posted on the Web site, a link off pay-per-click landing pages, and posted on the intranet for sales use. That way, every fresh story already has an attached plan and schedule for use.

Communicate to All, Often

Finally, make sure that anyone—either inside or outside your organization—who might come across a good customer candidate knows how to recognize it when he sees or hears it. Define for customer-facing employees and partners exactly what makes a great story for your organization. While sales reps may have a good grip on this, other customer-facing staff such as customer service may not. So, don't just say, "We need a manufacturing company using our Web-based service." Rather say, "We need a mid-sized manufacturing company effectively using our Web-based service to reduce turnover, lower overtime costs, and comply with labor-union requirements." Be specific!

Continuously reinforce not only that you're seeking stories, but what *types* of stories. Use regular communications avenues to alert all groups about the stories you need:

- Sales meetings
- One-on-one meetings
- Employee newsletters or intranet
- Partner/reseller newsletters and online communities
- Customer newsletters
- E-mail
- Sales or partner events

By taking a more strategic approach to story planning, your stories will not only be more effective, but you'll maximize your budget dollars —only investing in stories that will truly impact your promotional efforts. The next chapter goes into how to find customers to fulfill your wish list.

Chapter Take-Aways

- Match story development with actual company needs.
- Focus on quality and relevance, rather than quantity.
- Create an inventory of all current stories and keep it updated.
- Assess how current stories meet the field's needs, and what they still need to sell more effectively.
- Learn from current satisfied customers which titles made the buying decision and what factors influenced them.
- Create an actionable "wish list" of stories to pursue.
- Know how you plan to use each story.
- Communicate specific needs to all, often.
- Make sure internal and external people know how to recognize strong story candidates.

4

Step 2:
Uncovering Customer Successes

"Stories give life to past experience. Stories make the events in memory memorable to others and to ourselves. This is one of the reasons why people like to tell stories."

—Roger C. Shank, *Tell me a Story*

With a "wish list" in hand, it's time to round up your best customer candidates. More than likely, there are yet undiscovered customer stories within your organization; you just need to find them. Sometimes it requires wrangling leads from busy sales or account reps and outside partners or resellers who may be protective of those customer relationships. A number of companies are applying best practices in bringing customer candidates to the surface. The key: continuous motivation and communication with reps and resellers.

The second step in the Seven-Step Customer-Story System involves putting into place processes to consistently collect customer-story leads from internal and external parties, and directly from customers, as well as pre-qualifying customers as suitable candidates. It's particularly valuable information for marketing managers, business owners, or independent consultants in the position of finding the best candidates to feature.

Bringing Leads to the Surface

In a perfect world, your employees and reseller partners would deliver a steady stream of story candidates to marketing teams or customer-reference programs, and customers would readily nominate themselves to be featured. In reality, it can be tough–even when your employees, partners, and customers will play leading roles in those positive stories. They're too busy doing their day-to-day jobs to (a) recognize a success story when they hear it, or (b) pass that information along to someone in a position to capture the story. Usually, getting leads takes a more calculated approach.

For Liz Pedro of LANDesk (www.landesk.com), that means understanding what drives sales representatives and building mutually beneficial relationships. In 2006, Pedro joined LANDesk, a leading provider of systems, security, and process-management solutions. As Customer Programs Manager, she oversees the company's customer-reference program, which includes customer success stories.

Tasked with finding and producing one to two fresh stories a month, Pedro needed an ongoing supply of customer references and success-story leads from sales representatives and partners. Sales people are typically already well compensated, so the key was figuring out what incentives would get their attention. "You have to find that 'golden amount' or a hot new gadget that will motivate them," Pedro says.

Applying her creativity, Pedro chose to run regular contests. When sales reps submit leads, Pedro enters them into a drawing to win electronics such as Nintendo or Sony game systems, or gift certificates to Amazon.com or other online sites. The tactic typically results in a high volume of names in a short period of time. Of course, Pedro still has to qualify those leads as viable candidates, but it's much easier with a strong pool of leads from which to pull. After contests, she announces the winners by email and mentions them in the company's internal newsletter–additional recognition that they appreciate.

Pedro also attributes her success in collecting leads to relationship-building with sales people and being present at times when they talk about customers. First, she makes sure they all know her. She introduces herself in person whenever possible and communicates continuously with sales reps. She sits in on sales meetings and calls, and listens for any mention of happy customers.

Sources for Story Leads

To find candidates, start by identifying which customer-facing employees or external partners may know about customer successes. Consider several usual suspects:

Sales reps and account managers—The best sources of leads are sales reps and account managers. They're on the ground, working first-hand with customers. Most should know a customer's current happiness level, and whether the products or services have effectively met a customer's objectives.

Partners/resellers—Many companies, especially in the technology realm, deliver their products through a reseller or partner channel. Resellers may be the most appropriate source—especially if they added value and support that went beyond simply selling the product or service. Resellers will want to publicize the customer's success and their role in that success. Typically, the vendor company produces the story (and often foots all or part of the bill) but involves and mentions the reseller.

Consulting/services teams—Consulting, technical, or professional-services teams deliver services directly to a customer, making them well positioned to hear about customer successes and unique uses of products or services firsthand.

Support reps—Customers usually call a support line when there's a problem. However, problems may be minor and unrelated to other successes. At times, customers may relay success-related information to support reps. Make sure those reps know what to do when they hear a good story.

Customers—End customers have brought in your product or service for a specific reason, and expect results. And when they improve something internally, they may want to document and publicize that success. Customers may even nominate themselves as potential success stories, if they know you're looking for it.

Additionally, she tries to take care of any needs sales people have, quickly, in order to build their trust. She responds immediately whenever a rep needs a live-customer reference or other materials to support a sale. Her fast response builds goodwill, which in turn encourages sales people to help her out with references and success-story candidates. "Even if it's not my area, I try to help them out if they come to me for anything," she says.

Creative Ways of Finding Stories

Pedro's approach, which merges creative incentives programs with relationship-building, seems to be the winning combination in finding customer-story candidates. Kronos® Incorporated (www.kronos.com), a global provider of workforce management solutions, takes an equally creative, relationship-focused approach to finding its best customer stories: an annual customer awards program.

Founded in 1977, Kronos employs more than 3,400 people and serves customers in more than sixty countries. Over three decades, the company has built a reputation for its solid solutions and exceptional customer focus. Its annual KronosWorks conference brings together nearly 1,500 workforce management professionals, including current customers, prospects, and partners, to talk about industry best practices. It was this annual event that inspired Kronos to create an awards program to recognize customers using the company's software in innovative ways.

"Our customers wanted to hear those stories," says Michele Glorie, Senior Director, Corporate Communications. "They wanted to see some of their brethren being recognized for innovative uses of Kronos solutions."

In response, Kronos created its Best Practices Awards Program in 1999 to recognize organizations that achieve unprecedented value and success with their Kronos solutions. Since then, the awards program has built a momentum that has even surprised Kronos. Through 2006, the company had recognized fifty-three winners, about five or six each year. And each year, the number of applications increases for what has become a very competitive program.

"It's become kind of the Academy Awards of KronosWorks," says Charlie DeWitt, Vice President of Enterprise and Product Marketing.

"It's a very big to-do. Past winners present awards to new winners. Winners display awards on their desks and walls, and are proud to be recognized."

Award winners are featured as the main event of the annual conference, included in media outreach and captured in success stories, if they have clearance from their organizations.

Kronos began the awards program as a way to recognize customers' achievements, but in the process has found some of its best customer stories. Sales and service representatives, and customers themselves, all remain on the lookout for innovative practices that might be award-winning. DeWitt says a customer might not even realize his or her organization is being innovative, so Kronos relies on its own representatives and partners to be eyes and ears in the search for award nominees. As a result, Kronos has found and captured a number of compelling customer stories.

'Tell Us Your Story' Links

Increasingly, I see organizations directly asking customers, members, and other beneficiaries of their products and services to share their stories. From consumer-products companies to business-to-business to nonprofit organizations, many now actively solicit stories with self-service "Share Your Story" links on their Web sites. Apple created a link for this soon after the release of its wildly popular iPhone. Along with all of its customer stories, FileMaker software includes a link to "Tell us your story." On the nonprofit side, Girl Scouts of the USA asks former members to share their experiences for its alumnae program.

Toyota Motor Sales finds a self-service story link extremely effective in gathering stories for its owners' site (www.toyotaownersonline.com). The site serves as a customer community with valuable resources for current owners, including maintenance schedules and dealer, parts, and service information. Owners can also read "Stories from the Road," a collection of positive accounts submitted by fellow Toyota owners via a "Submit Your Story" link. The company added the self-service link when it became clear that customers wanted to talk about their experiences with Toyota. "Our Customer Relations department reports that owners call in to compliment Toyota on our products," said Jennee Julius, Advertising and Promotions Manager for Dealer Operations. "Basically, they are telling their story to the rep they're talking to. We felt this site would enable our customers to interact with Toyota in that way, as well as with other Toyota owners."

Toyota began collecting stories online in 2005, and now about seventy customers contribute their stories every month. On an online form, they indicate a vehicle type, a story topic (general or 100,000, 200,000, or 300,000 miles), a title, and then tell their stories in up to 3,000 characters and spaces. Once submitted, Toyota reviews and edits stories as needed before publishing some on the site. According to Julius, this gives customers a way to share their stories with Toyota, while also letting current customers read about other owners' experiences, either with the same vehicle or with a vehicle an owner might be considering. Those true accounts, straight from customers, are honest, believable experiences that reinforce Toyota's brand messages.

When encouraging customers to submit their own stories or story ideas, guide them with an online form that asks a few specific questions. That helps you categorize stories as you process them and ensures that customers provide certain important details.

Self-Service Story-Publishing Options

You have two options for publishing information that comes through "Share Your Story" links on your own site:

- Run stories as first-person customer accounts, with minimal editing.
- Create third-person, professionally written stories from customer-submitted information.

First, decide what's more effective for your format. It's somewhat of a generalization, but first-person stories seem more fitting for consumer products (electronics, laundry detergent, vehicles), while third-person customer stories are more appropriate for business solutions. Typically, consumers look for stories with qualitative details about other customers' experiences with products, services, or support.

Businesses have a greater need to justify purchases based on quantitative return on investment information. For the former, it's easier to take customer stories in their raw format and accomplish your goal. But the latter usually requires guidance from your marketing team or a writer to help customers measure results.

Likewise, consider maintenance and cost issues related to stories. If you go with first-person accounts, you'll just need a simple review process before publishing those stories. You have to make sure there's no profanity, complaint information (which can be forwarded to the relevant department for follow-up), or typos in the text. It's a low-cost, easy-to-manage process.

If professionally crafted stories more effectively convey the image or information you need to communicate, then consider a more formal format and process. You can take the information customers submitted, write it in third person, design it in your format, and publish it. Perhaps use a direct quote or two from the customer. If you plan to publish submitted information without additional customer interviews, ensure that you ask enough questions and collect enough on your initial online story form. Also, you will likely want a disclaimer to which customers agree online that indicates they understand the information will be published on your site, possibly with edits.

Or, you can use the online form as a first step in gathering information, and then follow up with additional questions for the customer to help quantify results. To decide the best approach for your company, consider your audience, and maintenance and cost considerations.

The Carrot or the Stick

In addition to these two examples, a number of creative ideas are in practice at organizations large and small to get employees, partners, and customers to contribute success-story leads.

Incentives for Internal and External Reps

We all love awards, gifts, a free lunch, recognition, positive publicity, etc. Give internal and external reps incentives that motivate them. Here are a few ideas in practice at leading global companies today.

Rewards—Like LANDesk's Liz Pedro, give reps who deliver a certain number of hot candidates rewards such as cash, ballgame tickets, gift certificates, or whatever will motivate them. A global technology company gives iPods to the best contributors of customer references to its reference program, where customer stories are one of several possible reference activities. Partners may also earn points in a company's partner program for contributing candidates.

Recognize top contributors—Honor top contributors at annual sales conferences or events, and in newsletters.

Make everyone famous—Reseller partners are usually driven by joint promotional opportunities. Give them mentions in the stories you create and opportunities to be interviewed by the media when applicable, allowing them to gain additional exposure. To that end, mention the partner in any press releases you put out about the customer.

Quotas

Some companies establish quotas for sales or account reps, or resellers/partners, to provide customer candidates for stories and other reference activities. One leading semiconductor company found that only about twenty percent of sales reps will provide references without quotas. The rest need a fire set under them.

Build Relationships with Reps and Resellers

Sales and account reps can be understandably protective of their customers and accounts. Reassure them that you will handle their customers with kid gloves, and do so. Also, if you're responsible for your company's customer story or reference program, establish relationships with sales reps. Make sure they know who you are and can trust you, so they're not handing customers over to a stranger. Depending on how large the company is, you may want to call new reps or resellers/partners to introduce yourself and the case-study program—a tactic employed by marketing/reference teams at even some very large companies. Be responsive when sale reps ask for other marketing-communications materials. In return, they will be more likely to respond with leads for you.

What's in it for Them?

Reps may forget just how valuable customer stories can be in the process. Remind them that if they provide candidates who turn into stories, they will have more stories to support future sales. Plus, their customers are often thrilled and honored to be featured, and may want to get the story out about their successes as well.

While it's not necessarily a sales or account rep's job to get customers to agree to be featured, he should be armed with basic information about the program if the topic comes up in conversations with customers.

Reference Programs

Many companies have customer-reference programs whereby they track customers who are willing to serve as references in some capacity. One customer may accept live calls from prospects, another might speak at a conference and participate in a customer story, and others may join in the complete range of reference-related activities. Even if you don't have a formal reference program, it's valuable to maintain a database, or at least a spreadsheet, which organizes customers by type, products, and services used, and the reference activities in which the customer is willing and able to participate. When someone in the organization needs a customer reference, or a reporter wants to interview a current customer, having an updated list allows you to identify a customer quickly to help maximize sales and media opportunities.

Reference programs also help companies with increasing participation in customer stories. When a customer is part of a reference program, he is effectively in an elite club of your best customers. You build closer relationships with them, perhaps include them in advisory boards or technology councils, invite them to VIP events, arrange lunches with them and executives, and give them opportunities to advance their own careers through speaking opportunities and articles. Naturally, closer relationships with customers can result in a greater willingness to participate in an activity such as documenting success in a story.

Whether you have an actual reference "program" or not, when you approach customers about being featured in a customer story, it's important to find out what additional activities the customer will participate in, and keep a record of it. As customers engage in certain activities, note the type and date to ensure you don't call on your best references too often.

Simplify Candidate Submission

Give sales and account representatives, as well as partners/resellers, specific ways to submit their customer-story candidates. To ensure that leads reach those in a position to act on them, create a very simple process and communicate it clearly and often.

FrontRange Solutions (www.frontrange.com) added a "Case Study Assessment" form to its customer-story process a couple of years ago. The company provides software and services to manage a wide variety of business relationships and customer service, including GoldMine® CRM software, IT Service Management, and HEAT® for service-desk management, as well as communications-management solutions.

FrontRange needed an organized way for front-line account reps, professional services consultants, and partners to submit their suggested customer candidates into the queue of stories for consideration. Before, reps recommended customer candidates to Marketing via emails, making for inconsistent and incomplete background on suggested stories. Often, busy sales reps provided just the company name, contact name, phone, and email without any other helpful details with which to determine the strength of the customer's story. FrontRange created the form in order to ensure it had the same complete background on every candidate.

Employees can find the form on the corporate intranet while partners access it on a partner-only site. The one-page form, filled out by employees or partners—not customers—simply asks for the relevant contact information of the submitter and featured customer, and some basic background: the solutions currently in place; length of time solutions have been in place; three highlights of how the solution(s) have impacted the customer's business; and whether the organization has yet indicated its interest or ability to participate in a customer story. FrontRange very specifically kept the form brief, knowing that reps likely wouldn't complete and submit anything longer.

The assessment form has eased the process for three distinct groups: reps and partners know where and how to submit candidates—and can do so quickly; the marketing team has relevant information to decide whether the story fits its current objectives and to reach out to customers; and the writer working on the story has all the contact information and key highlights to begin interviews, first with internal contacts and then with customer contacts.

Qualifying Candidates

When leads come in from internal or external reps, they are not likely story-ready. In fact, it might not even be a story that's valuable for your sales and marketing objectives at this time. Assess all incoming leads against your wish list. Does the customer fit in a slot you're trying to fill? If leads don't match your needs currently, they may in the future. Your requirements may change, and the customer's story may change.

The Pre-Qual Interview

If a customer looks good on paper, consider conducting a short pre-qualification interview to learn more. You should already have some basic background about the organization's history with your company, and the products and services the customer has used. Develop a set of questions that further qualifies it as a good candidate for a success story:

- What business objectives was the customer trying to address with the product or service?
- How effectively did the customer meet those objectives?
- What are the top 2-3 benefits the customer has seen?
- Are there any measurable results to tie to the product or service?
- Any great anecdotes about the solution in action?
- On a scale of 1-10, how would the customer rate its satisfaction level with the product or service?
- On a scale of 1-10, how would the customer rate its satisfaction with the vendor as a whole?
- Would the customer recommend the product or service to a colleague?

- Would customer contacts be willing to participate in a public customer story?

- Who in the organization would need to provide clearance to proceed on a customer story?

Characteristics of Potential Customer-Story Candidates

Some customers make for better customer stories than others. Here are some indicators that your customer is a good candidate to be featured.

The customer's really happy—and sees real business value!

Refer to your customer database or check with account reps to learn of any outstanding support or billing issues for a story candidate. Or find out directly from the customer in an informal check-in.

There's an interesting story to tell

Is your customer's story interesting to readers or the media? Maybe the customer has made significant strides in combating a pesky industry problem, or has a story that fits perfectly in with a hot topic in the media right now. For example, a CRM software company learned that the state of Arkansas leveraged its solution to spring into action and help Hurricane Katrina evacuees find temporary shelter, food, clothing, and even loved ones. The company created a customer story featuring the state's proactive approach, and then pitched it successfully to a leading trade magazine in the industry. The result: a human story showing how technology actually helped reunite families, giving the state government recognition for its heroic efforts.

The customer has qualitative or quantitative results

Ideally, you want to show specific results that have come from the customer's use of a solution.

Messages you want to communicate

At this time, is the customer's story aligned with messages that you want to communicate to your audience? It might be too early, or just not the right time, or the right amount of customer enthusiasm. You can always reassess again later.

As the featured organizations show, you don't need a large budget for incentives to elicit customer-story leads from internal and external reps. Rather, it requires creativity and consistency in how you communicate and encourage leads—and simple ways for your colleagues to submit them.

Chapter Take-Aways

- Offer sales/account reps and partners/resellers creative incentives to provide customer-story leads.

- Build mutually beneficial relationships with those in a position to provide story leads.

- Take care of any needs sales has, quickly.

- Recognize those who submit the most story leads.

- Try "Tell Us Your Story" links for customers to nominate themselves.

- Communicate frequently to all customer-facing staff and partners, as well as customers themselves, that you're looking for story candidates.

- Create simple ways for internal and external reps to submit leads.

- Pre-qualify a candidate's suitability with a short interview.

- Establish a way to track customers willing to participate in various types of reference activities, including customer stories.

5

Step 3:
Securing Customer Permission

"People are hungry for stories. It's part of our very being."

-Studs Terkel, author

Securing permission to feature your customers is an essential part of Success-Story Marketing. On the surface, approaching customers seems like a simple task. You ask, and if they're satisfied with your products or services, they agree. Yet, even with your happiest customers, it's rarely so black and white. Unless you're working directly with a business owner or leader of an organization, your contact likely can't provide permission without clearing it with other members of the organization first.

It's critical to gain all the proper clearances—before you begin a story. Otherwise, you risk going through the entire customer-story process, and then not getting customer permission to use the compelling story you created. Organizations today don't take use of their names, logos, or information lightly, and you have to protect your business—and above all your customer relationships—by securing customer permission upfront. Too many organizations simply take the word of their closest customer contacts as the green light in proceeding. However, executives, corporate communications, and legal reps for your customer company will all want to know about the story and ensure that participation will be a positive move. That often requires that you collaborate with your contacts to understand how the story can benefit both your organization and your customer. Unfortunately, securing permission to feature customers ranks as the top challenge for many organizations. Some companies cannot or will not share their stories publicly—even if it's purely a positive story about them.

This chapter covers the third step in the Seven-Step Customer-Story System. It looks at why customers participate and ways that you can approach them to maximize the outcome—and ultimately create a story that not only protects your customer relationships but enhances them. In short, it's about partnering with customers for mutual benefit.

Permission First

If your customers are satisfied, why wouldn't they want to showcase that success? After all, it just costs them a small amount of time, and they benefit from positive exposure and publicity with the vendor organization footing the bill. Getting customers to agree to participate can be as simple as a two-minute explanation and request, and a simple "yes," or it can be a years-long campaign involving numerous parties and departments.

Why Customers Say No

Getting big-name companies to go on record is the "Holy Grail" when it comes to references and customer stories. Yet, these are the most challenging customers to land. Likewise, financial companies and the federal government top the list of the most notoriously difficult organizations to feature publicly. Unlike small businesses, many have large legal teams, public shareholders, and far-reaching restrictions on how their names are used publicly.

Unfortunately, some have what amounts to blanket policies, either put out by legal or corporate communications groups, against endorsing products or services publicly. If a *Fortune* 100 company has hundreds of vendors, it may not allow *any* stories to be created about it due to the time that would be involved in participating in dozens of stories. At that rate, legal and corporate communications teams would be consumed with reviewing stories for vendor organizations.

And then there are liability issues. Companies worry that going on record as endorsing a vendor will come back to haunt them later in some way. Ironically, many of the organizations with blanket policies against being featured *in* customer stories actively create them *on* their own customers.

Depending upon the subject matter, companies also consider security issues when deciding whether to participate. They might readily be featured in stories about their sales-force automation software, but decline a request to talk about their data-security solutions or corporate network for fear of revealing details that could make them vulnerable to attacks. With issues such as identity theft, it's a better-safe-than-sorry attitude.

Even without widespread policies, larger companies may be selective in the stories in which they participate. Big companies like to be associated with other household names, so they might grant a request to another big name before agreeing to a small vendor's request. It's unfair, but businesses do what they think will help them get ahead and what's most worth their time.

Companies can also be concerned about protecting information that could tip off competitors about their internal best practices. Beyond that, larger companies are simply more restrictive in how their names and information are used (especially if they're publicly traded) or very controlled in managing their corporate images and messaging.

Small businesses may decline a request for some of the same reasons. When a small business or organization turns down free publicity, it's usually either extremely busy or trying to protect what they see as competitive information about how it does business. It's growing and may see your products or services as a competitive trade secret it doesn't want to share. In a way, you can take it as a compliment, but it's still frustrating when a happy customer won't talk about its success publicly.

Does Size Matter?

We're a society of name-droppers. We want to know what our favorite celebrities and leaders drive, where they eat or vacation, and what they wear. And by simple association, those places, products, and services are suddenly more attractive.

Business is no different. Those with whom you keep company say something about who you are as a business. In that regard, having known, established companies or brands as your customers, and letting people know, does bring credibility by association. Successful companies do business with other successful companies.

Everyone wants to create customer stories on big-name, *Fortune* 100 companies. Yet, a known name isn't always the best way to communicate with your audience. Prospective customers need to see themselves and their challenges reflected in your stories. While a small business might be impressed that you work with a name it knows, that small business can't necessarily identify with the challenges of a global corporation. In fact, small and mid-sized organizations may be turned off if it appears that you don't work with customers of their size and type. Unfortunately, they may believe that larger customers will get more attention from the vendor.

Ensure that stories appeal to your various audiences, not just in size, but also geographically, by industry, and any other differentiators that help prospects envision what it would be like to work with your company.

Steven Nicks, Partner and Co-founder of Phelon Group (www.phelongroup.com), suggests a way to get the big bang of the big name without having stories on those customers. "You can say who you work with, but you don't necessary have to have a story on them," he says. "So you get the benefit of those big names even without specific stories. Once you get to the actual story, relevance is more important than a name, but for that to be true you have to be past the name-dropping phase."

Also recognize that smaller companies may be sources for some of your strongest stories. "Sometimes the most innovative companies are innovative because they're small and nimble," says Stephanie Porter, Director of Relationship Marketing at Amdocs. "We discovered a couple of customers that are innovative, but not quite big-name yet."

Why Customers Say Yes

Your customers are extremely busy, so they're unlikely to simply participate unless something is in it for them. That doesn't necessarily mean discounts or other financial incentives. Many other things motivate customers, and these vary by customer.

Individuals at your customer company might be interested in documenting and publicizing the success they have achieved with your products or services, especially if your solutions contribute to the bottom line. Every year, managers are involved in budget planning. If they can show that a particular product, service, or vendor saves the department money, time, or improves business in other key ways, then the company is more likely to retain the solution. A customer story gives managers the documentation and justification they need to defend decisions.

Individuals also want to be recognized in their organizations for bringing in best-practices solutions that help a division or company do business better. A customer story showcases those successful decisions, giving the individual(s) involved positive internal exposure. These folks are proud to share their accomplishments at their current organizations, and may even frame your story in their offices! One IT manager I encountered credits participation in a success story for a vendor with helping him get positive internal recognition and a promotion to director level. And, contacts might take those stories along to the next employer to demonstrate how their leadership and decisions made a difference.

A story can also help an individual or company be recognized within the industry. If the story is picked up by a leading publication, both your organization and the customer benefit from the positive publicity. Smaller customers, with more limited marketing and PR budgets, often say yes for the free, positive exposure. Companies of any size go for it if they believe it will help them increase awareness in a targeted geography, publication, or market. I've seen customers featured in customer stories end up getting significant publicity in major media outlets, land new customers, get major industry speaking opportunities, receive awards, and more—all as a result of going public regarding their business practices.

Plus, customers want their vendors to succeed. While interviewing my clients' customers over the years, several times they have expressed hope that, by sharing their stories, they are helping their vendors succeed and stay in business. After the technology fallout of the late '90s and early 2000s, customers are genuinely concerned about the longevity of their vendors and want to do their part to fuel the vendor's success.

These are just a few of the motivations for participating in customer stories. As the next section discusses, it's important to read customers on a case-by-case basis to discover what motivates them and their companies.

Strategies for Increasing Customer Participation

Some creative, best-practices companies have found that "no" may not always mean "no" when approaching customers about story participation. They find ways around roadblocks with strategic approaches that take the customer relationship into full consideration.

At Amdocs (www.amdocs.com), a $2.4 billion dollar provider of customer-experience software and services, publicly showcasing marquee customers' success stories is extremely important to its marketing and PR efforts. "If we want to do something we think the press might also pick up, or for awards submissions, the bigger the name, the better," says Stephanie Porter, Director of Relationship Marketing.

In the Relationship Marketing team at Amdocs, all those focusing on customer-reference relationships have sales backgrounds—with good reason. The group approaches its big-name customers regarding being references just as it would if it were selling a product or service. "It's no different than a sales call," Porter says. "It's really about relationships." And just like sales, you have to have a strong value proposition to make participation worth the customer's effort. Amdocs does its homework, meets with all stakeholders, and plans the best approach for each customer it wants to include in reference and success-story programs.

The team focuses on a subset of the Amdocs' customer base. Though the customer base spans thousands of companies in fifty countries, the team identifies fifty customers who can deliver eighty percent of all reference activities. Amdocs sells heavily to this group, partners with them in reference activities and success stories, and makes sure they know they're appreciated for it. Virtually all customers in this group would be considered marquee names, yet the team consistently lands them for success stories.

"Every one of our customers says, 'We don't do publicity and we don't do case studies,'" Porter says. "But there's an angle for everything. The door may be shut but the window's wide open. You've just got to look for the windows since sometimes they're in the back of the house."

Open Windows

Porter and her group identify those openings by first meeting with all stakeholders monthly—product marketing, public relations, analyst relations, etc.—to all share what they've heard about top customers. Then, Relationship Marketing checks out all promising leads.

First, Porter's group must gain the trust of the account team for each customer to ensure everyone feels comfortable letting Relationship Marketing and the evidence team contact customers directly. And that respect continues throughout the process; Relationship Marketing always keeps account teams updated on activities with customers. The department also spends considerable time with the account team to understand the customer well. Then, an account manager makes an introduction to the customer contacts.

From there, Relationship Marketing talks openly with a customer about its current goals and objectives, not just the customer company's objectives, but also the individual contacts. Sometimes it takes a number of meetings to get to know them well, understand how they benefit from Amdocs solutions, and arrive at an acceptable agreement. The end goal: Understand what they are willing and able to do in terms of reference activity.

With all that homework, Relationship Marketing approaches each customer with a customized proposal for reference and success-story activities that the customer considers reasonable for them. The group takes care to emphasize for customers the win-win aspects of the partnership. What motivates one customer might not motivate another.

Perhaps the customer will speak at an event or participate in high-profile marketing campaigns that will help him or her achieve professional or personal goals, or get across the company's own corporate message to a new audience. "We get to know them very well and understand who within a company is looking to move up, or achieve other objectives, and might be willing to work with their corporate communications groups to make it happen," Porter says.

One Amdocs' customer wanted to establish itself as a thought leader on its continent, to be seen as at the forefront of its industry. In response, Relationship Marketing devised a plan with a series of activities to help the company build exposure and work toward its goal.

Amdocs' Stephanie Porter points out that *networking* opportunities remain the top motivator for customers. Amdocs hosts small events to bring together its top customer contacts. As few as five handpicked customers have the chance to compare notes and best practices, and learn from each other—an opportunity that can be difficult to find otherwise.

Representing Customer Interests

Because many customers use multiple Amdocs products, Porter's team must run interference between all the internal product groups and customers. "Maybe we've got fourteen products we think we can leverage with customer X," she says. "There's not enough of customer X to go around." Through internal meetings, the group prioritizes the products and types of reference activities that would deliver the greatest value for Amdocs with the least amount of customer effort. Relationship Marketing aims to minimize the time customers spend providing information, so Amdocs captures it once and then leverages it in many ways.

Customers often agree to only one reference activity initially, so the team considers what will be the most beneficial, whether that's a case study, speaking engagement, or press release, for example. Ultimately, the customer decides how much and what it will do. "If the customer says, 'What are the two most important activities to you?' we need to know the answer right there." If the customer is only willing to participate in one case study, Amdocs may create one story, but try to pull out smaller stories for specific uses. It's a challenging process, but Porter says it's worth it to keep top customers happy.

Motivators

Incentives pose a tricky topic when it comes to giving them in exchange for endorsements of your products or services. To both sides, it can feel like the customer's endorsement is being "bought," even if customers are genuinely happy with your solutions. In fact, few large companies give discounts in exchange for customer stories or other reference activities.

Fortunately, most customers prefer other motivators over discounts or monetary enticements. Again, a number of companies report that *access* and *involvement* motivate their customers most. They want access to your company leadership, their peers in the industry, and best-practices advice. And they want to be involved in your product roadmap and enhancements to products and services. If your customers have business titles, they may prefer meetings or events with the chance to interface with your executives, or participation on your advisory board. People with technical titles usually prefer participation on technical councils/boards where their product suggestions are heard and they have a chance to share ideas with their peers. Others might want the chance to be beta testers of new product versions. Giving customers access to your leadership, and involvement in your company's direction, strengthens relationships with your best customers, possibly paving the way for greater success in requests for customer stories.

As the Amdocs' example emphasizes, you have to listen to customers and figure out what motivates each one. In exchange for customer participation in stories published publicly, devise creative ways to meet their needs. Have the CEO call or visit your top ten customers, or invite your top ten to twelve to an advisory meeting. That kind of attention goes a long way.

Some companies choose to give customers a token of appreciation for participating. If you choose to do so, make sure it's not presented as an enticement upfront, but rather as a thank-you gesture after the project is complete.

One technology company, with small-business customers, gives featured customers Amazon gift cards as a thank-you for participation in customer stories, or a discount on a software renewal. The firm tells customers about the gift cards at the time they are asked to participate, which results in a high participation rate. It's an attractive offer for these small businesses. If you choose to offer something like this, position it as a token of appreciation so as not to seem like you're buying the customer's endorsement.

Customer Motivators

From startups to global enterprises, every company struggles with getting customers to go on record. Here are some ideas in practice at companies today for encouraging customers to participate in customer stories:

Access and involvement–Surprisingly, the #1 thing customers want is access and involvement–access to your execs and involvement in your product/service roadmap. Create ways for your top customers to interact with your organization on a deeper level.

Co-marketing campaigns–Create a few co-marketing campaigns for the customers you most want to feature. The focus: How successful the customer is, and one of its steps to success has been using your solutions.

Joint-benefit story angles–If possible, find a way to tell your story and the story that your customer wants to tell the public.

An evolving relationship–Move customers through a series of communities of increasing importance, from user groups to advisory boards and tech councils.

Customer fame–Make individual contacts famous with a campaign highlighting the customer's best practices.

Rare exceptions for the most coveted customers–In the sales process, you can consider offering training or other services in exchange for reference activity. If you do choose to extend discounts at that time, then ask customers to participate in multiple reference activities.

Reminders about publicity possibilities–If your solution saved a department money, increased sales, or improved customer service, for example, approach the department head. A story could be very valuable in demonstrating the success of that individual and helping him justify having made the investment.

Awards opportunities–Everyone wants to be recognized for success. Take every opportunity to submit customers for awards and PR opportunities, and they will be more willing to participate.

Persistence–Some of the world's largest companies spend *years* building customer relationships, gradually involving the customer more in joint marketing activities (speaking at conferences and panels, accepting reference calls, and then customer stories).

Alternatives when you can't go public–Internal-only or unnamed use of customer stories may be the only way to get some customers on board.

Each customer may require a unique approach. Know what you can and can't offer.

Involve Corporate Communications

During the customer-story process, when I hear the word "legal," I cross my fingers. When a customer's attorney or legal team is involved in providing permission to be featured in a story, or later is brought in to review the draft, momentum often stops. Corporate attorneys have the best interests of their companies in mind, and are doing their jobs, but sometimes doing their jobs means declining a request.

From experience, I recommend contacting corporate communications or public-relations teams, after your primary customer contact has agreed to participate in a story. Their jobs involve promoting the company favorably—and a customer story can tie in nicely with that goal.

PR representatives understand the request and the benefits of participation, especially if you plan to pitch the story to the media yourself. Effectively, it's positive publicity that the customer's PR team doesn't have to chase on its own.

So, after getting the agreement of your primary contacts to be featured, suggest a joint call with one of the company's corporate communications contacts to discuss the request and next steps. Your customer's own internal PR contacts are usually more successful in convincing legal and other parties to approve the request for a customer story.

An Angle the Customer Can't Refuse

Along those same lines, try to find a way to accomplish your communications' goals and your customer's goals with one story. Do the products and services you provide contribute to successes and initiatives that the customer wants to make known publicly? "We often want to tell our story and we fail to think about how we can tell our story in a context that also is exciting to our customer being featured in the story," says Steven Nicks, Partner and Co-founder of Phelon Group. "If the customer is solving a problem for their clients, and your solution is helping that, there would be a benefit for them. That would excite them."

Uncovering story angles that motivate customers requires conversations among your company, your immediate customer contacts, and corporate communications to settle on an angle that will benefit all.

Set the Expectation Early

Many companies find it valuable to plant the seeds for customer stories early, even during the sales process. Some do it informally, while others bring it into actual negotiations. Jeffrey White, Vice President of Sales at KnowTia, maker of OasisCRM software (www.oasiscrm.com), informally mentions the possibility of featuring a customer during the sales process. In fact, he sees it as an effective *closing* strategy.

"I'm telling them, 'If I exceed your expectations, we'll be coming back to you for a success story in two or three months,'" White said. "That says to them, 'We're dedicated to making sure the software will be successful for them.' It's the number-one way to close a sale."

In this case, the customer isn't bound to anything, but is merely given the expectation that (a) the vendor is committed to making the customer's experience successful and (b) that the customer might be asked to participate in documenting that success later on, if willing and able.

While KnowTia discusses success stories informally, other companies bring up the topic of being a reference or a customer story as part of actual sales negotiations, and may even write it into the sales contract. In this scenario, the customer story can become a bargaining chip for the vendor. If the potential customer pushes for price concessions, the service or product provider might request a success story in exchange.

This gets tricky because a customer may not be able to follow through with that, even if it's in the contract. Landing an actual customer story depends upon the customer's happiness level, amount of success with the products or services, and corporate permission, all of which can vary depending on what's happening day to day. That's why some feel that including customer stories in sales conversations may force a company to concede something in hopes of getting a story that may or may not pan out.

"You're only going to want customers to talk about you if they're happy and if you've delivered value. So trying to contractually oblige someone to talk about you at a future date simply means you're probably going to have to give something up in terms of your sale price without any definite gain," Nicks says.

Plus, you never want to buy a customer's endorsement or obligate contacts to talk about you. As mentioned earlier, this tactic simply plants a seed. This can be particularly effective for smaller organizations selling to a larger customer. The small company wants the chance to reference a customer with a known name while the larger organization is pushing for breaks in the sale. If the customer agrees to a story early on, it can decrease the risk of the customer declining later because the organization has already gotten what it wants in the sales negotiations.

However, if you do choose to bring the customer story into the sales contract, make sure the relationship takes priority over such contract details. Include clear language about what a customer story is to help customers understand what they are agreeing to.

The Art of Asking

Once you have names of story candidates in hand, here's a typical process for approaching existing customers about participating:

Choose your Timing Wisely

A number of times I have helped clients capture stories on some of their best, longest-running customers. Yet the interviews and information were flat. The customers knew they were benefiting from the product or service, but they had used the solution so long it had simply become the way of doing business. They couldn't remember the pains or problems they experienced before, or why they had chosen the vendor, and had lost the early excitement associated with the vendor. Worse yet, in some cases the person involved in bringing in the vendor had moved on to another company, so we could only piece together part of the full story. A story is most powerful when you can show before-and-after differences, and it's tough to do so if the person you interview doesn't know what things were like before your solution.

You'll get the best emotion and most beneficial details by carefully choosing just the right time to feature customers.

You can also feature a customer too early. Understandably, businesses are eager to capture stories on happy customers, especially those with more recognizable names. But going after customer stories too soon also makes for flat information. When interviewed prematurely, customers cannot provide the details and anecdotes that make for interesting stories.

The best time to capture a customer's story completely depends upon your products or services, and what you want to communicate. Customers may experience results from day one or years may pass to see the full results. Choose a point in the relationship when the customer has had enough time to see actual results from your solutions. But don't wait so long that the customer loses that early excitement or has forgotten how bad things were before you came along. Worse yet, those who championed and chose your solution or company may leave the organization. When that happens, it's tough to reconstruct a strong story.

For many companies, capturing the pains and problems of the customer's life before the new solution is one of the most interesting aspects. What was the organization hoping to remedy or improve? Why did it choose your solutions over others?

If you want that early "selection" information, but customers don't see full results for a while, you might consider capturing the story in two phases. For example, a marketing or search-engine-optimization campaign might take a while to show measurable results. In this case, you can capture an early story that talks about the customer's goals, why they chose your company, and the experience of working with you. Then later, go back and update the story with the powerful metrics that really demonstrate results.

Check for Red Flags

The customer may have been happy last week, but a lot can happen in a week. Check with those closest to the customer, or your customer relationship management software, for any new developments that could influence the customer's happiness level, such as service or support issues.

If anything looks like a red flag, either have sales or account reps, or the partner company, contact the customer to assess the current situation. When in doubt, wait a while and assess again in a month or two. You want the strongest story possible, so if there's any question, focus on taking care of the customer's issues and look for other customers to feature.

Approach Customer Contacts

As you begin the process of securing permission, start with your main customer contacts—those who know and understand your solutions the most. Get their buy-in first since they'll be the people involved in interviews and reviews, and can help pursue greater corporate permission. If your contacts are owners or executives, they probably have the authority to make the decision about participating.

Typically, it's most effective if the person closest to the customer at your organization introduces the idea of participating. That's usually a sales or account representative. That individual has the best relationship with the customer, so it makes sense to leverage those strong relationships first, rather than a stranger calling out of the blue. The sales or account representative should simply find out if the customer is open to talking with someone about participating. Then, the sales or account representative introduces the customer to whomever manages your customer stories or reference program, and shares any helpful information about the customer's current situation.

Follow up quickly with that customer contact. If you wait too long, he or she may not remember discussing it with the sales rep. Verbally communicate your interest in "featuring" the customer. Highlight the joint promotional aspects and any other benefits that are relevant. Here's where you have the chance to get to know the customer a little more and find out how this can help him, or if she is interested in access or involvement opportunities such as advisory boards, tech councils, or beta testing. Provide the basics of what's involved: how much of his time it will take and how the story will be used. Gauge the customer's interest level. If she is open to it, plan to follow up by email with written information to arm the customer with the materials to help pursue broader corporate permission.

Send Your 'Pitch Packet'

Before truly agreeing, customers need to understand exactly what it's all about. That includes everything from what a story is and looks like, to how much time it takes on their end, to how it will be used once complete. Create a "pitch packet," typically a set of materials you can email, which gives them all the information they need to decide and to forward on to other decision-makers. Here are some suggested pieces of the pitch packet:

Samples of other customer stories—Provide a couple of current stories in their final format. If you've never created any before, go online to companies you respect and whose stories you like and pull those as samples of what yours *will* look like. This helps customers envision how their stories will look when complete.

One-page description of the process and use—Create a one-page document that describes your process, from end-to-end, and includes how the story will be used. Also include key benefits for the customer. Keep it fairly brief. *See inset for an example.*

Success-Story Process—ABC Company

Customers want to know what's involved in being featured in a customer story. Create a one-page document that describes your process succinctly. Here's an example:

Thank you for your interest in ABC Company's Success-Story Program. ABC Company success stories highlight customers and the benefits and results they have achieved with our products and services. It's a great opportunity for you to document and measure your successes, and gain positive exposure for your best-practices approaches.

We aim to keep the process quick and convenient for all involved. Here's what's involved in a success story project:

Interview–*A writer will contact you to schedule an interview at your convenience. The writer walks you through a set of questions regarding your experience with ABC Company solutions. Typically, interviews take 30 minutes to one hour.*

Draft review–*You will receive a draft of the success story for your review. Circulate the draft to those individuals who need to review it at your company, make edits and changes in the draft, and send it back to ABC Company. ABC Company will then provide a clean draft for final approval.*

Final approval–*Sign the release form or have it signed by an authorized company representative, and return the form to ABC Company.*

The total time estimated for customer participation is 1-1.5 hours, with the interview taking the majority of the time.

Success-Story Use

You will receive an electronic version of the finished success story. It will be posted on our Web site and will also be used in sales opportunities, sales training, newsletters, direct marketing campaigns, and public-relations opportunities.

We appreciate your consideration regarding participation in our success story program. Please contact _____ for additional information.

Interview questionnaire—Many customers appreciate seeing interview questions ahead of time and having a chance to prepare, especially if you plan to ask for details regarding measurable results.

The release form—Some organizations choose to use a legal release form that customers sign indicating their permission to use the finalized story (more about this in Chapter Eight). If your organization uses a release form, give customers a copy ahead of time so they know what they will be agreeing to.

Move toward an Answer

When talking with your main customer contact, find out who else needs to be involved in the decision. Ask for the names of those individuals and their departments. Agree on the call whether your customer contact will speak with those individuals about participating in the story, or if you, as the vendor company, will assist with that part.

If the customer contact seems exceptionally busy, or doesn't press to handle this, offer to make those inquiries yourself. However, sometimes your contact may feel strongly about being able to make the case for participation more effectively than you could. Perhaps the best combination is the customer forwarding the pitch packet with his stamp of approval on to relevant contacts, copying you, and then you follow up with the relevant contacts by phone. If the request is left to customer contacts, it's easy for them to get busy and for the request to move off the radar screen. Stay in touch and "politely persistent" as you pursue permission.

A Reverse Approach

Ideally, you secure customer permission *before* proceeding with a story. However, sometimes vendor companies move forward without prior clearance in hopes that the customer will approve the story later on. It's a risky move, but if it's a high-value story, perhaps it's worth investing the time and resources in hopes of securing permission later.

For example, say a customer speaks at an industry event or one that you sponsor, delivering what amounts to an oral success story. It may even be on tape. Usually accompanied by PowerPoint slides, customer presentations can be excellent sources of rich detail about how they are using your solutions. Afterward, turn that information into a written success story. Present it to the customer as documentation of what he or she presented and ask if it's possible to get permission to use it publicly. At times this works because customers don't need to participate in any additional interviews. Or, you can create a story based on information provided by your own contacts that are close to the customer. Craft a quote or two for the customer, or leave a blank spot for the customer to insert a quote during his or her review. You've done all the work and are simply asking for final approval. The same goes for creating success-story-oriented press releases. Create the release and then run it past the customer.

Polite Persistence

Customers do benefit from vendor stories featuring them; however, it's still essential to remain "politely persistent" throughout the entire process. The story is not likely at the top of your customer's priority list. During the process, never show a hint of impatience, for these are your best customers. Any employees or contactors involved in capturing customer stories must remain just as agreeable in any dealings with customers—even if it takes months to secure an interview or obtain final story approval. Keep the process collaborative and always respect the customer's time.

Some companies spend months or even years trying to get customers to go public with details of their experiences, either in speaking opportunities, printed customer stories, or audio or video content. Sometimes it's as easy as simply asking, and other times takes a team to devise a strategy and years of relationship-building. Use this information to formulate an approach that works for your unique business and each customer you approach. Also realize that it may not be worth your time to continuously chase after a customer who's not coming through, and instead focus your efforts on those you can feature.

When the Customer Won't Go Public

What if you diligently try every avenue and your customer still says no to a public story? Or worse yet, you go through the entire process and the company doesn't approve the final story for use? Fortunately, alternatives exist to a public-use story.

Unnamed

The unnamed customer story has a bad reputation. No one really wants to feature a "global semiconductor company." You want the credibility that goes with telling the market that you work with a *specific* global semiconductor company. But you can't name customers who don't give you permission. In fact, it's a good idea to get a customer's permission even if you simply want to list its name on your Web site.

In reality, the unnamed customer story goes further than you think. If part of a customer story's purpose is education and validation, the rich information in even an anonymous case study provides prospective customers with insight on how you deliver your solutions in a customer's setting and the results that customers see.

"From a credibility standpoint, I find that names are better, but you can still have a credible piece without the company name," says Brian Carroll, CEO of InTouch (www.startswithalead.com) and author of *Lead Generation for the Complex Sale*. "We've still done case studies without using customers' names, but providing enough information that it appears to be a real company."

Don't automatically discount an unnamed, or anonymous, customer story. Unnamed stories, if detailed, still educate prospects and validate your products and services.

Acumen Solutions (www.acumensolutions.com), a business and technology consulting firm, has created dozens of unnamed customer stories. This approach originally began out of necessity. "We help clients transform their businesses and often they don't want their customers to know that they didn't do it themselves," says Donita Prakash, Chief Marketing Officer. "Especially if they are technology leaders, they don't like to name names of business and technology consulting firms they use."

Acumen Solutions still finds those stories very effective in its sales and marketing efforts. By using anonymous stories, the company can capture more stories, more quickly. With no long approval cycles to secure customer signoff, that speed and ease results in a larger base of stories to support sales. In sales meetings, chances are, Acumen Solutions has a story that matches the prospect's situation down to the industry, business problem, or type of department.

After each project, client leads at Acumen Solutions write up summaries and submit them to Marketing. When possible, they calculate return on investment details themselves, or even collaborate with clients to capture that. Publishing numbers becomes easier when the customer knows its name won't be connected to the figures. The marketing staff then places those stories into a standard case-study format. Some are published on the public Web site while a larger number go on the company's intranet for sales access.

Limited Use

If customers cannot or will not agree to full public use of a story, sometimes they will grant limited use. That can mean specifications on where and how the information is used, as well as for how long. You can still squeeze a lot of value out of a limited-use story. Start with finding out what the customer's concerns are, and then propose a fitting limited-use option.

Here's one example:

A business-to-business software company developed a story on one of its marquee clients, which happens to be a *Fortune* 100 company. While the customer contacts agreed to participate, the legal department declined, saying the company does not disclose its business practices in detail. The software company quickly came back with a limited-distribution proposal that respected the customer's concerns.

The vendor suggested that it would not publish the story on its Web site, but instead would create a PDF file of the story that would only be used in press kits, and in one-on-one sales opportunities—either emailed directly to potential customers or printed and handed out. The customer accepted those terms, but countered with others. The vendor could only use the success story for six months. And, if media stories resulted from the press kit, the featured company would grant fifteen-minute interviews to be included as part of larger stories, but would not agree to complete feature stories about their business practices and use of the B2B software. The arrangement respected the customer's wishes and concerns, but still allowed the software company to leverage this valuable customer name as a reference.

Some Amdocs' customers have agreed to internal-only story use. At Amdocs, completed stories are available in a database for employee use. If customers only grant internal-use permission—sometimes even when the customer is unnamed—the story is flagged as such in the database. In some cases, that means employees can't download, copy, or email those stories. Instead, they read the story online and commit it to memory so they can recount it only in one-on-one sales conversations with prospects. This option captures customer results in a story format that sales representatives can use, but respects customers' wishes for non-public use. Or in some instances, stories will be marked that they cannot be shared with some of the customer's specific competitors.

Amdocs' Porter stresses that it's still important to get permission from customers even for limited, unnamed use. She also recommends implementing measures that help ensure that stories are not used outside of the boundaries of agreements with customers. Also, check in with customers periodically to ensure they are still comfortable with the story-use arrangement.

When approaching your customers regarding participation in stories, understand their needs, concerns, motivators, and current goals. Then take all those into consideration while still meeting your objectives for the customer story. Doing so may require more time and thought, but it pays off with a strong story that your customer will approve.

Chapter Take-Aways

- Customers decline participation in stories for a number of reasons: liability, security, competitive reasons, or time considerations.

- Sometimes a story on a big-name customer will best resonate with your audience while other times a more appropriate story on a lesser-known customer is best.

- Customers say "yes" to story participation for positive publicity, internal documentation of success, professional gain, or to support a vendor's success.

- Do your homework to understand the customer's background and relationship with your company.

- Approach customers about participation as if you are selling them an idea.

- Ask them at the right time, when they are happy and not experiencing any problems.

- Listen to customers' needs and concerns, understand what motivates them, and respond with a win-win arrangement.

- Send customers details about what's involved and how stories will be used.

- Get the customer's full corporate permission before starting a story.

- Consider other options if you can't get full public use.

- Stay politely persistent throughout the process.

6

Step 4:
Intelligence Gathering

"Stories are the single most powerful weapon in a leader's arsenal."

—Howard Gardner, Harvard University

Y̶ou can't construct a compelling customer story without all the right building blocks of information. Information gathering is critically important to the quality of a story, and it begins long before the interview. It starts with a solid understanding of the subject matter, a sense of the goal of each customer story, thoughtful interview preparation, and then focused, yet flexible, interviews with end customers.

This chapter details Step 4 in the Seven-Step Customer-Story System, gathering all the information you need from relevant parties to create powerful stories. Whether you're handling the interview and writing, or managing a writer in the process, this chapter helps you understand how to prep for interviews, create interview questionnaires, identify the best interviewees, and manage the logistics of your interviews so that you collect the information you need and keep the process painless for customers.

Study Featured Products/Services

Before embarking on a customer story, the interviewer (usually also the writer) must have a very firm grasp of the subject matter. You can't interview on or write about something you don't really understand. The interviewer needs to know the subject well enough to ask relevant questions, and to sound intelligent in conversations with customers. Whether you use an in-house writer or a contract writer, customers expect that person to have a good working knowledge of the products and services being discussed.

If the interviewer/writer is new to the subject matter, she should begin by studying the products and services that will be featured in stories. Most companies keep their most current information on their Web sites. Writers should read through all company, product, and service materials, and view demos, to get a sense of the language and terms the company uses in talking about its solutions.

Customer-Story Objectives

It often helps for writers to talk with one or more parties at the company as well, and collect important information that isn't apparent from the Web site:

- What's the objective for the customer stories, and how will they be used?

- Who's the audience for the stories—business or technical individuals, or both?

- What's the competitive climate, and what are the competitive differentiators of these solutions?

- What are the top objections and concerns you hear in the sales process?

- Are there certain key themes that should be repeated across different stories, such as ease of use, flexibility, results, etc.?

- What types of measurable results do customers usually experience with the solutions?

These are just some of the questions that help interviewers/writers understand the goal of customer stories and begin framing their questions.

Interview Questionnaire Prep At-a-Glance

1. Study the products and services to be featured.

2. Know the objectives for the story.

3. Create a general set of interview questions.

4. Study background and details on the customer to be featured.

5. Tailor the general set of questions with some specific to the customer.

6. If customers request, or you think it will enhance the interview, send questions to interviewees ahead of time.

The General Interview Questionnaire

With all the company, product, and service homework behind her, the interviewer/writer should create a "general" set of interview questions. Type up a comprehensive list of questions based on the information you want to elicit from customers. This will serve as the base set of questions for all interviews. Writers with years of interview experience may not feel the need to be so formal about the interview questionnaire, but there are a couple of good reasons to do this.

First, customers often want to see the interview questions ahead of time. Some companies routinely send customers questions before interviews, while others send them when customers ask. If customers have the time and desire to review questions ahead of time and think about answers, it always results in a stronger interview, especially when you're requesting measurable results. You might suggest to customers that it will help them prepare, but whether they actually do so is up to them.

Your organization may create customer stories frequently or only occasionally. If a contract writer is involved, and a month or two has passed, that writer may need to refresh his memory about the subject matter. If those interview questions are saved in a document, the writer has them ready to go and doesn't need to take the time to reinvent them all over again. It's also a good idea for multiple people involved in customer stories to have the general interview questionnaire on file so they can also email questions to customers when asked.

Customer-Specific Study

Every customer story is different, and it's essential to find the unique aspects of each. When a customer is ready to go, then prepare for that specific story. Review the company's Web site to understand what they do and for whom, how long they've been in business, number of locations, and anything else that seems relevant to the story. Customers always appreciate when you know something about their business before the interview begins.

As preparation, try to talk with the person closest to the customer at the vendor company, whether that's an internal sales or account representative, professional-services consultant, or an external reseller/partner. Find out helpful information such as how long the company has been a customer, which products and services the company has used, what they were looking to accomplish, any highlights of their use or experience with the solutions, and any other details that will help you understand the customer's situation. It's also a good time to find out about any sensitive areas to avoid in the interview, such as a rocky implementation or support issues. From there, determine the specific angle that will best support your objectives. For example, in one story you might focus on implementation speed and ease, while in another feature how a solution helps the customer comply with industry regulations.

The Customer-Specific Interview Questionnaire

Once you collect background on the customer, go back to that general set of interview questions you already created and customize it with some that are specific to that customer and the angle you're pursuing. Then save it as a separate document. That ensures you gather the general information you need for every story, as well as the unique customer-specific details that make each story different from another—and more interesting.

Interviewing

Interviewing is both art and science. The art comes in how you interact with customers, put them at ease, and encourage them to provide information. The science comes in what you ask and how you ask it.

Your Interviewer

Customer stories are not objective pieces of journalism. They are initiated by vendor companies as success stories featuring only happy customers. However, the information is true. When interviewing customers, should the interviewer be someone from the vendor company, or a third-party individual or firm with some distance? Some contend that third parties are more effective in gathering information from customers. It's like this: Say you bake homemade cookies for a friend. You want to know whether the friend liked the cookies, and how much. It's awkward for you to ask the friend directly just how great your cookies tasted, and on a scale of one to ten, how she might rate those cookies. Similarly, it can feel a little strange for an in-house interviewer, business owner, or independent consultant to ask customers about their products and services.

Hence, a third-party interviewer may be more effective. Even though the third-party writer has been hired by the company, there's a perception of distance on the part of the customer, who may be more willing to open up than if he's talking to the company's PR manager. The distance that third parties bring may also enhance the interview questions and outcome of the story because internal contacts can be too close to the subject matter.

At times, someone within the vendor company or PR firm may want to conduct customer interviews for specific reasons. The company could be interested in the information for product development, or PR reps might want to assess how well the customer handles interviews. If the writer does not lead the interview, always at least include the writer in the interview, and allow him to ask any questions as needed. Writers usually know what they need to make a complete story. There have been times, as a contract writer, that I have been asked to be silent on phone interviews with customers while someone else asks the questions. When the interview was over, if I still had questions, I was asked to email them to my contact, who would try to get answers.

Inevitably, someone would have to go back to the customer for that information, which makes the vendor company look disorganized. Let the writer be part of the process so that he can participate and enhance it.

If someone other than the writer conducts the interview, always include the writer. Writers usually know what they need to create a compelling story, and need the opportunity to ask their own questions.

Interviewees

Choose your interviewees wisely to maximize the impact of your stories. One software company I began working with found their customer stories ineffective in the sales process. They soon realized the source of the problem. Those they interviewed for customer stories were often technical people, the actual users of their solutions. But the decision-makers, the people who read the customers stories, were in business roles. What the technical people saw as beneficial information wasn't necessarily what business decision-makers wanted to know. And vice-versa—an IT manager will connect with and respond more to what another IT manager has to say about a solution. It's a common oversight in customer stories—a disconnect between the information the company wants to capture and what the interviewee can actually provide. The interviewee should be in a similar position to those prospects or customers who will read the completed story.

Sometimes, it makes sense to interview and quote multiple subjects from one organization, such as when you're trying to show how a solution can be used throughout an organization. IHS (www.ihs.com), a global data and services provider, interviewed seven people to show the use of one solution across an entire team. The benefits and value of the solution varied across the different subjects, from field employees to managers, so the multiple voices demonstrated that versatility. I recommend only interviewing multiple subjects when it will truly enhance the story because extra interviews adds to project time.

Don't underestimate the importance of talking with *enthusiastic* customers. There's a clear correlation between a customer's excitement and the strength of the resulting story. The customer company may be seeing phenomenal results with a product or service, but the customer contact can still be lukewarm on an interview. Maybe it's just the individual's personality, or maybe a back story exists you don't know (maybe the main contact originally wanted to go with another solution). Customer pre-qualification should include some questioning that allows you to gauge their enthusiasm. If they just don't seem excited, you may want to move on to others.

Participant Limits

Your customer contacts are extremely busy, and most of the time, your customer story isn't the highest priority. The interview must be short and focused. Including too many people on a phone interview can slow it down and impact the quality of information you collect. That includes parties on your side as well as on the customer side. In either case, only include those who can really add to the call, or who need the information for other purposes, such as a PR representative planning a press release.

On the customer side, often one contact can cover the entire story—a person who chose the solution and has owned the project throughout. In that case, it makes sense to interview that one person. Often, a manager made the purchase decision, but other team members actively used the solution or were involved in the project. Then it's valuable to talk to both parties to understand why the customer needed something like this and why they chose your product or service, as well as the day-to-day use and benefits. Contacts across multiple departments may have different experiences of the products or services. You can either include multiple parties on one call, or schedule separate interviews for each. Usually take a cue from customers regarding their preferences. Sometimes the multiple customer contacts on a call help jog each others' memories, resulting in better information. However, a joint call with all the different voices may take an hour for all parties, while a call with each separately would only require fifteen to twenty minutes for each. Regardless, try to limit calls to two customer contacts, or three at the very most. On the case study where I interviewed seven contacts for one story, I talked to each separately because all used the product very distinctively and were tough to schedule at one time.

Sales and account reps, or partners, as well as product or marketing managers, may want to join in customer interviews. It's one thing if they want to just sit in on the interview, and another if they plan to actively engage customers in questions. Too many voices can take the interview off course. One active speaker from your company plus the writer would be the max on the vendor side during questioning. You can always open the call to questions from other parties at the end.

General Questioning Techniques

You may have heard the golden rule of interviewing: ask open-ended questions, or questions that interviewees can't answer with just "yes" or "no." Specific questions really depend upon your subject matter and product/service, but here are some ways to begin open-ended questions:

Can you describe...?

Let's talk about...

Tell me about...

Can you name the top three benefits of...?

What was/is the impact of...?

How has [whatever is impacted] changed with the product or service?

In what ways...?

How does it allow you to...?

Can you please share an example or anecdote of a time when the solution...?

Specific Questioning

After completing the interview preparation, you should have all the necessary information about the featured solutions and customer to begin crafting interview questions:

- A strong understanding of the solutions to be featured
- Background on the specific customer to be interviewed
- Knowledge of the angle and goal for the story
- Interviewees identified

Next, your interview questions should elicit exactly the information you need to create the story that will best meet the stated objectives. Specific questions vary by company, but in customer stories here is a logical flow of questioning:

- The customer's business/organization
- The need for the solution
- The decision process
- The delivery/implementation/ramp-up process
- Description of the solution in action
- Details of results
- Wrap-up/Future

Following are some suggested questions for each of these areas:

The Customer's Business/Organization

You've already studied the customer's Web site, but the Web site doesn't reveal everything that could be helpful for the story. You need to understand the company's current challenges, goals, and the market and climate in which it operates.

Q: *How long have you been in business?*

Q: *How many locations do you have?*

Q: *How many employees?*

Q: *What are some of the organization's current goals and challenges (fast growth, new markets, mergers/acquisitions, regulations to comply with...)?*

Q: *What are some of the objectives of your department or business unit at this time?*

The Need for the Solution

This helps put the entire story into the context of the customer's goals. The customer has needs and you have solutions.

Q: *Tell me about some of the business objectives or challenges that led you to look for a solution of this type. What were the drivers?*

Q: *What were the ramifications of not having a solution to address or accomplish this?*

Q: *Can you quantify the problem in any way?* (Help the customer here by suggesting something that might be measurable in regard to their challenges—lost time, lost money, poor customer service, and so on. Feel free to dig more if the customer isn't specific. Specifics on the "before" help you show measurable results later.)

The Decision Process

Prospective customers are particularly interested in how other organizations approached the decision-making process.

Q: *How did you hear about our solution?*

Q: *How did the selection process go?*

Q: *Which products or services did you evaluate? (You may not name actual competitors in the public story, but this information helps sales reps and other internal parties understand how and why customers selected the solution.)*

Q: *What was most important to you in a solution?*

Q: *Why ultimately did you choose our solution? Which specific features were most attractive?*

The Delivery/Implementation/Ramp-Up Process

This part varies depending on what you offer. Complex technical products may take months to implement, while other solutions and services are immediately ready for use. If you're interviewing people in higher-level business roles, they may not be the best to address some of the technical questions like this. Consider multiple interviews with people familiar with different aspects of the solution.

Q: *How did implementation go?*

Q: *Who was involved at your company?*

Q: *How did the vendor or partner/reseller assist with the process?*

Q: *Were there specific integrations or customizations required? At multiple locations?*

Q: *How long did it take? Did that meet or exceed your expectations? How would that have compared to other options you considered?*

Q: *Was there training involved? What was your experience of the quality of the training?*

Q: *How quickly did your staff pick up the solution and begin using it?*

Q: *What has been the feedback from them regarding the ease of use?*

The Solution in Action

Next, get into the details of how the products or services are used and/or delivered.

Q: *How many people use the product/service, or were involved in the process?*

Q: *Across which departments and locations?*

Q: *In what key ways do you use the solution the most? (This encourages them to tell you what's important to their organization.)*

Q: *Do you take advantage of X capability, and how does that provide a benefit? (Here, create several questions around your specific capabilities to draw out details.)*

Details of Results

Here are some suggested areas of questioning to help draw out measurable results. Refer to the section later in the chapter (Capturing Results) for more guidance. Of course, what you ask completely depends upon your product or service, but these should help you think about ways to craft your own questions.

Time-savings

Q: *At what points do you find you are saving time? How long did the specific event or process take before as compared to now? Across how many people? (Customers may share actual time-savings, or they may translate this into a percentage. Assess their comfort level in how to best present these results. They may not want to publicly reveal that something took one hundred hours before and now only two.)*

Q: *Are you able to do the same amount of work with less staff, or get more done with the same staff? Please explain.*

Productivity

Q: *Have you reduced downtime or outages?*

Q: *How much faster can employees find the information they need to do their jobs?*

Q: *How much quicker were you able to get a problem solved or solution in place compared to other options?*

Sales/Marketing

Q: *Are reps able to make more calls or visits in a day?*

Q: *In what ways does this enhance your competitive advantage?*

Q: *How much have you increased site traffic/open rates/conversions?*

Q: *How has it allowed you to create and support new revenue streams?*

Operational Efficiency

Q: *How much does the solution reduce training time for new employees?*

Q: *How has it increased employee satisfaction?*

Q: *Has employee turnover improved?*

Customer service

Q: *How has the solution enabled you to change the customer experience?*

Q: *About how much faster can you get orders out the door now?*

Q: *Has it reduced the time to resolve customer issues?*

Q: *Has the solution helped improve customer-survey results? By how much and in what areas?*

Q: *How did it lower customer turnover, or increase customer retention?*

Safety

Q: *Has the solution helped reduce the number of safety incidents?*

Q: *Did it reduce insurance premiums?*

Compliance

Q: *Which regulatory requirements does the solution assist you in meeting, and how do you know you are meeting them more effectively?*

Q: *Have you experienced fewer fines, or lower costs related to consultants employed to assist with compliance?*

Q: *In what ways is it helping you better meet regulatory requirements?*

Financial Impact

Q: *What hard costs were eliminated by bringing in this solution?*

Q: *Have time-savings allowed you to save on labor costs, either by reallocating staff or eliminating the need to hire? By about how many full-time employees (FTEs)?*

Q: *Was the project completed on time and on budget?*

Q: *Has the solution allowed you to eliminate or delay the need for purchases? What is the estimated cost-savings of that?*

Q: *How does it allow you to capture more revenue?*

Q: *How does it enable you to shorten your accounts payable times or improve cash flow?*

Q: *At what point did the solution pay for itself, and at this point, what is the estimated return on your initial investment?*

Wrap-Up/Future

Q: *Ultimately, how does our product/service allow you to...*(insert the customer's original goals stated at the start of the interview)?

Q: *How do you plan to expand your use of the solution in the future, and what additional results do you expect?*

Q: *Is there anything else that we haven't talked about that you would like to add?* (Keep your pen handy! This may elicit some of your best customer comments.)

Interviewer: *Thanks so much for your time and valuable input.* (Then let the customer know how you plan to use this information, and when he can expect to see content to review and approve.)

Capturing Results

For most organizations, documenting results is the ultimate goal of the customer story–while also the most challenging information to get. Many customers simply don't track this information, and if they do, they may not be willing to give it up. They're afraid their competitors will know their latest and greatest trade secrets, or don't want to publicly give too much credit to an outside consultant, product, or service. You have to decide for your organization what type of results information is most significant for your audience.

Qualitative vs. Quantitative

Nearly all organizations hope to capture specific measurable results, with dollar figures, of using their products or services. Many prospects need that hard evidence to justify purchases, especially for high-dollar solutions. In customer stories, there are two ways to present results: qualitative or quantitative. Qualitative refers to general benefits experiences. The customer says he is saving time or money, realizing efficiency or productivity, selling more widgets, doing business better, has a more secure network, or whatever the benefit is—without measurable details.

Quantitative takes it a step further by attempting to put numbers on those benefits. How much faster is a process now as compared to before? How many more sales are closed each month? How much more data can a server crunch in a given amount of time? Have incidents of downtime decreased? Ideally, the customer can translate those numbers into actual dollar figures. How much are new sales worth? How much money does a business save by reducing a process by two hours a day? How many people, at what salaries, can be reallocated to other areas due to automation? How much have regulatory fines or equipment replacement costs been reduced?

Every customer should have at least qualitative results, and hopefully some quantitative, to share. Even if they can calculate specific numbers, they may be hesitant to reveal them. They might be interested in measuring results to support internal decision-making, but not willing to release those details publicly. At times, you may have to choose between creating a customer story that lists detailed results numbers but leaves out the customer's name, or a story that includes the customer's name but leaves out detailed results numbers. Choose based on your specific goals and plans for the story. If you plan to use it mainly in the sales process, perhaps specific metrics are more valuable than the customer's name. In PR, editors want a name.

Also, some solutions lend themselves much more readily to quantifiable results. For example, it might be tough to quantify the increased productivity achieved with better employee training compared to consulting services that increase Web site traffic. In the first case, customers have a sense they are saving time and doing business better, but find it hard to measure. In the second example, if they know their Web traffic statistics from before, they can compare it easily to current traffic to determine an increase.

Timing Stories to Improve Results Details

The previous chapter discussed the importance of timing when approaching customers about stories. Your timing also makes a difference in your ability to elicit details of customers' results. Here are a few guidelines for timing your stories:

If Non-Quantifiable Benefits Support Your Objectives

Many businesses capture customer stories before measurable results are available because there's already a story to serve their needs. Here are some themes that are valuable even without measurable results:

- Featuring the selection process, and why a customer chose your solution over others
- Implementation speed or success
- Ease of integration with other systems
- To establish credibility by featuring a well-known name
- To demonstrate important capabilities the solution enables or problems it solves
- To show work in a key vertical or geographic market
- The solution solves a common problem
- Highlight features/capabilities of a new release in a product
- Showcase custom integration—a unique and impressive mix of solutions working together seamlessly
- Demonstrate regulatory compliance

If Measurable Results Are Your Main Goal

When metrics are what matters, analyze your customer base and talk with sales reps to understand about how long it usually takes for customers to notice quantifiable results with your products or services. When is that point in time? Decide on a "sweet spot" that represents the typical amount of time this usually takes. Track new customers and set reminders to check back at this point in the relationship to pre-qualify them as possible candidates.

Just remember, if you create the story early with non-quantifiable metrics, you can circle back later to collect metrics to enhance the case. Likewise, you can always update any story with measurable results with better, fresher metrics later on.

A Pre-Solution Assessment

In the midst of their busy workdays, customers can have a tough time putting a finger on measurable results. They often need guidance in this process. Determining quantifiable results largely hinges on knowing the situation before, so a successful tactic is helping them recall the details of the previous situation, and then encouraging them to compare previous to current. That's why it's advisable to perform an assessment for customers before bringing in a product or service.

Establish Success Metrics

First, get your team together and create a set of "success metrics," all the possible ways that your customer might realize a quantifiable benefit. Sales probably has a good handle on the issues and challenges customers faced before–always a good area to focus on in determining results. Then look at the benefits that your company or solution provides. Between the customer's previous challenges and the benefits you offer, you should be able to come up with a solid set of success metrics.

Assess at the Outset of the Relationship

Using your success metrics, create a list of questions relevant to your business and what you provide for customers that attempts to measure specific areas. Don't make it too extensive. Go over the questions in person or on a call with customers, recording answers–before providing any products or services. This gives everyone a valuable baseline metric on which to compare results.

Before-and-after questioning is the best way to elicit measurable results from customers.

Reassess

Then go back with the exact same questionnaire at the point when most customers see benefits. That allows you to compare changes on a before-and-after basis, and see measurable results. It's not only valuable data for customer stories, but also helps you and customers clearly see the impact of the solution. Look for the most impressive gains between the before and after. If they look good, there's your candidate for a customer story.

Lisa Koss, President of International Advantage—*Leading across Cultures* (www.intladvantage.com), performs a pre- and post-climate survey on each project. The organizational development consulting-firm works with leaders of medium-sized to large companies in cross-cultural environments as they navigate organizational change, team development, or individual development. International Advantage consultants typically go on site to assist clients over the course of several months to guide them in reaching the pre-established goals.

In large organizations where many variables affect bottom-line improvements and the benefits of more effective teams can be hard to measure, International Advantage's climate survey asks customers about their feelings on certain areas by indicating "dissatisfied," "very satisfied," or varying levels in between. Conducting the survey before and after allows the firm to show the specific areas where customers have improved. This was particularly valuable when Koss created a customer story about a major project. The client improved significantly in seventy-five percent of the areas surveyed. Instead of nebulous discussion about improved productivity, the survey showed exactly where and how much of a leap the customer made.

ROI vs. Payback Period

Ideally, you can show the return on investment (ROI) of your solutions or the payback period, the amount of time it took for the customer to recover the initial cost of the investment. Mainstay Partners (www.mainstaypartners.net), an independent third party that helps companies capture the value of technology investments, defines ROI and payback period in the following ways[13]:

---

13. *ROI Aliases, An IT Measure with Many Names*, Mainstay Perspectives, 2007

ROI—The net benefits captured divided by the initial investment expressed as a percentage (*always* represented as a percentage). If the solution costs $5,000 and the company ultimately saves one full-time position at $35,000 per year, then that's an ROI of 700 percent, for example.

Payback period—The amount of time necessary to recoup the initial investment, represented in months. Again, if the solution costs $5,000 and the company saves $35,000 per year ($2,916/mo.), then it takes less than two months to make up the initial cost.

Some solutions lend themselves more readily to measurable results than others. Pursue quantitative results, knowing you may have to settle for qualitative at times.

Suggesting Metrics

If you know what other customers have experienced in the way of measurable results, you can suggest numbers and see how that compares to the customer's situation. Here's a sample question that applies to shipping automation software:

Q: *Some customers have found that they reduce the time to process a shipment from five minutes to about one minute per shipment. Is that about what you have experienced? Across how many packages per week?*

Customers will either confirm they experience the same savings or will share other numbers. With that, you can calculate a time-savings per week. Then you can take it a step further to find out if that allows them to put off hiring or reallocate staff to other activities. If they have seen such benefits, then try to quantify that in terms of labor costs saved, for example.

Interviewing Tips and Hints

Here's where some of the art comes in—in how you manage scheduling and conducting interviews with customers, from dealing with different personalities to logistics.

Putting Interviewees at Ease

Some customer contacts may be experienced and familiar with being interviewed for media stories or customer stories, while others have never been interviewed before. You'll encounter varying comfort levels depending upon the customer's personality and interview experience. Make the process as easy and accommodating as possible.

Schedule interviews when it is most convenient for customers. Ensure all parties are clear on the correct time zone and how long the interview is expected to take. As previously discussed, many customers appreciate receiving the list of interview questions ahead of time, which helps them prepare. It also eases their concerns about having valuable answers to your questions. Clarify whether you will call the customer directly or arrange a conference call.

From my experience, about ninety percent of the time, customers are there and ready for the interview at the agreed-upon time. Occasionally, something comes up that requires the customer to reschedule. If you get the customer's voice mail, leave a message with your number asking him to return the call to proceed with the interview or reschedule. The customer may just be running a few minutes behind. Regardless of what happens, *always be gracious and patient* with the customer. I've had customer contacts reschedule five times before we could finally proceed. Remain agreeable and understanding, and work with the customer's schedule and limitations. Sometimes that means calling her at night on her mobile phone after a long day at a trade show in Vegas (if she asked you to call then), or while she's driving to work.

Begin every interview by thanking customers for their time and willingness to share their experiences with the featured solutions. Remind them what the conversation will cover and how the story will be used ("Today we're here to talk about..."). It doesn't hurt to confirm again that the contact has secured company approval to participate, and ask who will need to review the customer story when completed. Always keep your tone and questioning friendly, yet professional.

Flexible Interviewing

Interviewing requires the interviewer to be flexible to the contact's personality and the information as it unfolds. When it comes to personalities, there are two extremes: the over-talker and the under-talker—

both of which make collecting information a challenge. The over-talker tells the story from his perspective without waiting for you to ask questions. It's up to you to control the direction of the conversation—politely—in order to get the relevant information. Whenever you have an opening, interject questions that steer the conversation back to where it needs to go.

Usually more challenging, under-talkers answer questions reluctantly and in as few words as possible. You may need to ask one question several different ways to get the answer. It helps to be as specific as possible. Here's an example from my own experience:

Q: *At what points are you realizing time-savings with the solution?*

A: *It saves us quite a bit of time throughout the day.*

Q: *What are some of the daily tasks that the solution streamlines for you?*

A: *It really helps by automating administrative tasks.*

Q: *Which administrative tasks does it automate?*

A: *The process of converting quotes to orders.*

Q: *How did you handle this process before, and how do you do it now with the solution?*

A: *(Customer describes process.)*

Q: *How long did it take before to convert quotes to orders, and how long does it take now?*

Each question gets increasingly more detailed until the customer finally offers some specific, measurable data. Sometimes you just have to keep asking to get what you need. However, pay attention to the customer's responses and ease up if it seems as though he is frustrated with the line of questioning or doesn't know the answers.

At times, customers won't have answers readily on hand during the interview, and may offer to get back to you with numbers or other details. In theory that sounds like a good idea, however, customers rarely track down that information and get back to you after the call is complete. They are busy and the customer story is not usually at the top of their lists. At times, I've tried including one or two questions for additional detail in the draft that customers see. Again, many times they do not address those questions during the draft review. If you are asking very detailed questions requiring specific numbers, for example, it's advisable to send customers the list of questions ahead of time and alert them about figures you're requesting.

It's also essential to remain agile to the information customers provide and the direction of the conversation. You may know the angle you want to pursue at the outset of the interview, but when you get on the call, there isn't enough "meat" to support that original angle or the customer may not want to tell the same story you do. You have to balance the customer's actual experience, and what contacts are willing to discuss, with your own story needs.

Handling Negative Comments

Customer-story interviews allow you to have an open dialogue with customers about their experiences with products or services. Within that framework, they occasionally open up about some of the less-than-positive aspects of their experiences. Usually, they're not too major. Otherwise, why would the customer agree to be featured in a success story? Almost always, that information can be taken as suggestions for improvement. When customers share this type of feedback, thank them and assure them that you will pass it on to the relevant parties. *Always* do this. When a customer is taking the time to be featured for her positive experiences, she trusts that you will also listen to suggestions or grievances.

The Phone is Your Friend

In a typical customer story, chances are your business is in one location and the featured customer in another city, state, or even country. Multiple contacts at the customer company may be spread across different locations. Then, the in-house or contracted writer may be in an altogether different place. Most often, it's perfectly acceptable, preferable, and certainly much more cost-effective to conduct interviews over the phone. Most businesses are very accustomed to doing business over the phone and email, and a phone interview shouldn't detract from the amount of detail you collect. In nearly a decade of developing customer stories for companies, I have conducted hundreds of customer interviews and only a handful have been in person. At times, visiting a customer's site would enhance the story. It might be valuable if you're creating a longer feature where details about the physical location and how solutions play out in those locations will truly add to the overall piece. But most often, explanations, photos, and diagrams enable writers to envision the setup without actually seeing it.

Conference Calls

When planning phone interviews with multiple parties, find out if call participants will be in one location on a speaker-phone together, or if they are in multiple locations. If parties on the call are dispersed, arrange a conference call. I personally like the "reservation-less" conferencing lines where no prior scheduling is required. The service I have (www.ReadyTalk.com) gave me a number that's all my own to use, a host code for me to enter, and a participant code that I send to others. I simply email all participants this number or send a meeting invite with the details. With the reservation-less service, I can even pull together a conference call on the fly.

International Phone Interviews

International interviews present varying levels of difficulty depending on where you are and where customers are. Time zones, foreign languages, and heavy accents all make it challenging. I've conducted phone interviews (separately) with an engineer riding a bus in Moscow, with an IT manager walking down the street (amidst non-stop car horns) in Bangalore, India, and at 10 p.m. my time to reach someone in Singapore. While interesting to connect with people on the other side of the world, issues related to international interviews can detract from the information you collect.

Before scheduling a call with an international customer, find out from the person closest to the customer how well the customer contact(s) speak your language and how heavy the person's accent is. Someone may be fluent in your language, but the accent is so thick you can't understand him well enough to conduct an interactive conversation. That's the primary determinant. If you can't understand each other, or the customer answers questions in just a few words, then you won't get very far.

You may decide it's better to have someone conduct the interview in the customer's native language, and then have the interview translated into your language from which to create a customer story. You might even end up translating the customer story in multiple languages, but ensure that the interview is conducted in a way that the interviewer and interviewee can both understand clearly.

If heavy accents are the main barrier, consider sending the customer a written set of interview questions that she can answer in written format and email back. Since it's not interactive like a phone conversation, ask detailed questions and encourage the customer to answer questions in two to three sentences, as he would on a call. Otherwise, his answers may be too brief to piece together a strong story.

If time zones or thick accents make live interviews challenging, collect customer information via email as a last resort.

Make sure you schedule calls for the right time zone, and don't always trust what the customer contact says is the time difference. She may tell you that it's five hours ahead of New York, but that may be during one part of the year and not another. Always double-check times on one of the free handy Web sites with international times:

www.worldtimeserver.com (my personal favorite)—This one has a nice "Meeting Planner" link at the top that shows you exactly what time it is in your location and another location at a certain future point.

www.timeanddate.com

www.timezoneconverter.com

www.worldtimezone.com

Also, find out whether an international call is subject to international calling codes. Places such as Puerto Rico are not considered international when called from the United States. If your call is, in fact, international, there are more options these days for affordable calling.

If you make international calls frequently, check into Voice over Internet Protocol (VoIP), services such as Skype, or a calling plan with affordable options to the regions where you call. For less frequent international calling, per-use calling codes may be your best bet.

Time Limits

You need details from customers, but you have to be as efficient as possible with a customer's time. Customer story interviews usually last anywhere from fifteen minutes to an hour. If you're interviewing multiple contacts separately, then each interview will likely take less time. One interview with one or more parties to collect all information means more time for the call. If at all possible, keep interviews to an hour or less. Any more than that takes too much of a customer's day. When scheduling an interview, let customers know about how long it will take. At the start of each interview, ask how much time the contact has. Watch the clock to ensure you never go beyond the agreed-upon amount of time.

Recording

Customer interviews can include complex details, especially with technical subject matter. Even though customers will review their stories for accuracy and other edits, it's important to ensure the information is as correct as possible when you present it to them. Inaccurate information looks unprofessional and takes more of the customer's time to correct. Recording interviews helps ensure that you capture the customer's information verbatim.

Laws regarding the recording of conversations vary depending on your location. Some places require the consent of only one party on a phone call, while others require consent of all parties. But when interviewing your most valued customers, it's a matter of courtesy rather than law to ask for permission to record the conversation. Just make sure customers know why you're recording the call and how you plan to use the recording. For example, I ask, "Do you mind if I record the call to assist with the writing process?" Ninety-nine percent of the time the customer doesn't mind or ask any additional questions. Some ask whether the recording will be used in any other way, or agree under the condition that it is not used in any other way.

If sales reps or account managers plan to listen to interviews for insight on the customer experience, let customers know that the recording might be shared, but only internally. Many companies now record interviews and post sound bites of those conversations on their Web sites. However, customers know ahead of time about this use and have given specific permission for it.

When I first started developing customer stories in the late '90s, I used a mini cassette recorder with mini tapes that hooked to my phone. At a rate of about four to five interviews per week, I soon had a drawer full of tiny tapes. I kept them for years just in case I needed to verify information later. Since then, technology and my recording method have moved into the digital age. By capturing an interview in electronic format, you can more easily jump around to different parts as you listen to interviews, more readily share the recording with other parties internally, or post it in audio format online. Digital recorders come in all shapes and sizes. You simply hook them up to your phone for recording and then download audio files to your computer.

Whether you actually transcribe interviews verbatim is up to each company and writer. It can take extra time and resources to create transcripts, so don't do so unless you really need them. Many writers refer to their notes and just use the recording as backup verification regarding details or quotes.

Effective interviewing demands a solid understanding of all featured parties and the subject matter, careful attention to question design, and both patience and flexibility as you interview customers. The result: Rich information with which to craft your stories.

Chapter Take-Aways

- Ensure interviewers/writers have a solid understanding of the solutions to be featured.
- Create a general interview questionnaire to serve as the basis of all interviews.
- Study the customer's business, history as a customer, and highlights of the customer's experience with your products and services.

- Tailor your general set of interview questions with some specific to the customer to be interviewed.

- Talk to enthusiastic customers.

- Choose interviewees that match the audience that will read the story.

- Limit the number of participants on calls.

- Help interviewees compare before-and-after situations to determine measurable results.

- Be patient, gracious, and flexible when it comes to customer interviews, and ensure interviewees feel comfortable throughout the process.

- Be flexible on interviews as information unfolds.

- Always pass on any suggestions for improvement or grievances the customer shares.

- Plan well for international calls.

7

Step 5:
Creating Compelling Stories

"If you're trying to persuade people to do something, or buy something, it seems to me you should use their language, the language in which they think."

—David Ogilvy in *The Art of Writing Advertising*

Some movies you watch over and over. Some campfire stories you can't wait to tell again. And some books you can't put down.

What makes a narrative compelling? A powerful, engaging story. Stories entertain us, help us develop societies and social bonds, and teach us. From our first books such as *The Little Engine that Could* to law-school case examples, stories help us learn important concepts and principles, and commit them to memory because they are put in a context we can understand.

Stories also educate us about the impact of a nonprofit's work or the way a financial advisor helped a family achieve its dreams. That's where customer stories stand apart from testimonials and other forms of communication. Nothing else draws in a reader like an engaging story. This chapter highlights Step 5 in the Seven-Step Customer-Story System, Creating Compelling Stories. It examines what makes stories compelling and your options in presenting information in the way that will best achieve your organization's objectives.

Tried-and-True Story Technique

Engaging stories typically follow certain patterns. With a similar flow of information and details, they help us associate with the people and organizations featured. Greek philosopher Aristotle is attributed with originally defining the three-act story structure that is the framework of most stories:

Setup—We are introduced to the characters and the setting.

Complication—The characters encounter some sort of challenge.

Resolution—The characters either triumphantly solve the problem, or they succumb to it.

The book *Made to Stick* calls it the "challenge plot," whereby a main character overcomes challenges and succeeds. This simple organization has become the foundation of dramatic writing, and plays out in numerous popular stories: *Star Wars, Hamlet, The Matrix, Lord of the Rings, Wizard of Oz,* and *The Odyssey.* Whether for a blockbuster movie or your next customer story, this story organization helps audiences get to know the characters, associate with their challenges, and then cheer them on to the desired resolution.

Customer stories lend themselves perfectly to this classic structure. Organizations and the people within them face real challenges, and with the help of solutions, they triumph over adversity. There are obstacles to overcome, and in the end, the organization is better off than it was before. To be compelling, a story must carry readers through those three stages. Audiences want to understand who the featured company and people are, why they needed a change, and how a resolution was effectively applied. Your next customer story doesn't need to be the next Great American Novel, and probably should not sound as dramatic as the quest for the Holy Grail, but this story structure greatly enhances readability.

Character Development

Effective stories help us connect with the featured people and organizations. For a reader to be engaged in the story, he needs to understand the characters in a human way. What are the characters struggling with and why is it so important to them to find a better solution? When you read, hear, or watch any story—fiction or non-fiction—you'll notice that good stories give you the chance to get to know the main characters. You may not like them, but at least you understand them, associate with some of their character traits and challenges, and want to know the outcome.

In customer stories, characters play out in the form of people, organizations, or both. If individuals are the beneficiaries of the product or service, as with eHarmony.com or The Make-A-Wish Foundation, then the story must introduce us to those individuals so we get to know them. When an organization is the featured character, the business entity takes on some classic human traits. It has goals and dreams, setbacks, ups and downs, make-or-break points, and so on. It's important to build a picture of the characters for readers, however, you don't need to talk at length about them. Weave in information about the company or person throughout, and make sure it's relevant to the story you're telling. It helps us understand the person, and places the story in context. The fact that a business has grown to three locations is not necessarily all that fascinating in itself. But it becomes much more intriguing when we hear that the owners, a refugee family from a war-torn part of Ethiopia, started the business with the money in their pockets.

Success Stories vs. Case Studies

The Don't-Miss Definitions section clarified the difference between success stories and case studies. As a reminder, a success story is an overview of the customer's experience with your products, services, or company. Case studies, usually two or more pages, go into more specifics about one or more customers, providing greater detail about certain aspects of a customer's experience. Instead of an overview as in a success story, a case study often goes more in-depth regarding use of products or services. However, most organizations call their customer stories case studies, success stories, customer profiles, or a number of other names, without regard to these specific definitions.

Success Stories

Various audiences respond best to the "overview" format of a success story. Phelon Group notes that within enterprise-level companies, "C-level" individuals (chief executive office, chief information officer, chief operations officer, to name a few) prefer summaries of this sort.[14] They don't want a lot of detail, but rather prefer to see a big picture of stability and results from vendors with whom they may enter into relationships. They expect others to have conducted the in-depth due diligence on all the details.

Decision-makers in sales roles may also lack patience for lots of detail when considering vendors. Many business owners fall into this category as well. They're too busy for many details, so they want to know the basics of how a solution will work for them. Can you do the job and do it well? Success stories can be effective for nearly anyone involved in a purchase decision.

Generally, executive-level decision-makers prefer the overview found in a success story, while managers and technical staff prefer the additional detail that a case study provides.

Case Studies

Case studies are most appropriate for decision-makers looking for more detail about specific aspects of your solution, such as technical specifications or business results. When evaluating technical solutions, those in technical positions want to know more about the time and challenges of integration, how a solution works with other solutions, scalability, ease of use and maintenance—all issues that will impact the tech person's daily job. Non-technical decision-makers, such as managers, may want the in-depth results of another customer's experience. Often judged on the success or failure of the decisions they make, they are looking for slam-dunks. All expenditures should ideally improve the bottom line. Companies that provide high-dollar, high-risk, enterprise-level solutions sometimes take the additional step of creating

---

14. *Success Sells*, Phelon Consulting Services, 2004.

detailed return-on-investment or total-cost-of-ownership case studies. There are firms that specifically do this type of analysis—and math—such as Mainstay Partners (www.mainstaypartners.net), which specializes in measuring the value of IT investments for companies.

Even in case studies, stay focused on customers and their experiences and avoid talking in generalities about your products or services. Other marketing materials such as data sheets and white papers provide the general product or service detail that customers want. Case studies can also feature multiple customers, however, most companies stay focused on one customer in a case study and leave examples of multiple customers for other marketing documents such as white papers.

Get to know your audience and how much detail they need to support their decisions. From there, determine whether a success story or case study will meet the need. The goal, in part, is to minimize the need for prospects to talk live with your current customers. If they read a success story and still want more detail about another customer's experience, then consider case studies.

Select a Story Format

Whether your organization plans to create success stories, case studies, or both, stories can take various formats. What's best for you depends upon how the story will be used and the audience. Here are some options:

Traditional

Try typing "customer success story" or "customer case study" into an online search engine, and actual customer stories created by companies come up. Explore some of those links to see how different organizations format their customer stories. Many follow a traditional flow with classic subheads: "Company" or "Background," "Challenge," "Solution," and "Results." They may not have those exact headings, but something similar. Many companies began using this format early on, and it is the most common format today. With this clean organization, readers know what's coming in each section.

However, because it's so common, this format may not be as engaging for readers as other approaches, especially for audiences who frequently read customer stories as they evaluate products or services. Just like a direct mail piece or a Web site, a customer story should be designed in a way that stands apart and draws in readers. Plus, those subheads don't communicate anything specific to readers hoping to skim the story for highlights.

Pros: Readers clearly know what to expect when they read each section. This format easily lends itself to short, as well as long, customer stories.

Cons: It's a bit formulaic and may not stand out as much as other formats. Non-specific subheads don't cater to audiences looking to skim stories.

Feature-Story Format

Increasingly, organizations are turning to other ways of presenting customer stories, such as a "feature story" format—more like what you see in magazines. Information may still follow the same progression as the traditional format, but it's not grouped into standard Challenge-Solution-Results subheads. Rather, a feature-story format employs journalism techniques such as a strong lead sentence or opening paragraph, and descriptive subheads as it moves along. This engages readers from the start and allows them to gather more of the story from the headline and subheads than the subheads in a traditional format—resulting in a more skimmable document. Because stories are written more like journalism pieces, they may more effectively catch the attention of editors at your targeted publications. For examples of this style, visit Z-Firm, LLC at www.zfirm.com.

Pros: Descriptive subheads make the story more skimmable, while a feature-story look can be more attractive to the media.

Cons: This format can require more skilled writing because the information has to flow more smoothly as a cohesive narrative, instead of being contained in standard Company-Problem-Solution-Results sections.

Breakdown of the Customer Story: Traditional Format

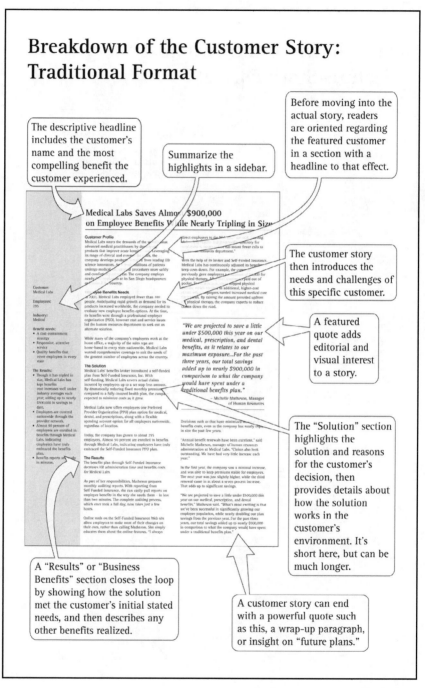

Before moving into the actual story, readers are oriented regarding the featured customer in a section with a headline to that effect.

The descriptive headline includes the customer's name and the most compelling benefit the customer experienced.

Summarize the highlights in a sidebar.

The customer story then introduces the needs and challenges of this specific customer.

A featured quote adds editorial and visual interest to a story.

The "Solution" section highlights the solution and reasons for the customer's decision, then provides details about how the solution works in the customer's environment. It's short here, but can be much longer.

A "Results" or "Business Benefits" section closes the loop by showing how the solution met the customer's initial stated needs, and then describes any other benefits realized.

A customer story can end with a powerful quote such as this, a wrap-up paragraph, or insight on "future plans."

See the full text of this story in Appendix A.

Breakdown of the Customer Story: Feature-Story Format

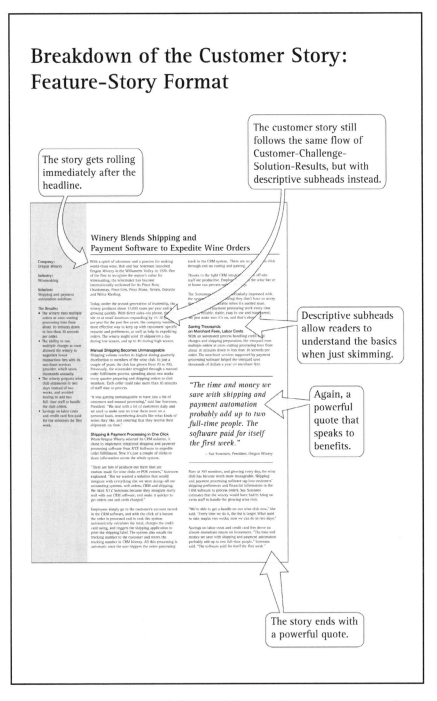

The story gets rolling immediately after the headline.

The customer story still follows the same flow of Customer-Challenge-Solution-Results, but with descriptive subheads instead.

Descriptive subheads allow readers to understand the basics when just skimming.

Again, a powerful quote that speaks to benefits.

The story ends with a powerful quote.

See the full text of this story in Appendix A.

First Person

For business audiences, most customer stories are told in third person. *The company* was trying to achieve this or that. Some organizations or consultants choose to present stories in the voice of the customer, speaking in first person, in "I" or "we" terms. It results in a completely different effect to write stories for business audiences in first person. This can be very effective with some audiences, and easier for some companies to manage. You see this most often in cases where individuals or consumers are the audience, rather than businesses. For example, a number of life coaches and business coaches use first-person customer stories to show how a customer benefited from coaching services. It has a certain authenticity to it. This shifts the emphasis from the featured company to the featured interviewee or person. It's an engaging, effective approach, particularly if the customers you feature hold prestigious titles. There's a certain credibility that goes with a high-level individual backing you in this way. The individual writes it from her perspective, indicating what she hoped to accomplish, the experience, and the results. If the individual agrees, the person's full name and possibly business name would be attached, or you could just attribute it to the customer's first initial and last name.

Guide Customers in Providing Information

In producing first-person customer stories, customers shouldn't simply write their own accounts without guidance. For stories to be effective for your purposes, they should include some key points. Create a list of questions or topics that you give to the customer to answer in the story, and some guidelines on length. Let them know you may edit the story for space or clarity. Or, you can ask the customer the questions yourself, and create a first-person story that the customer reviews and approves.

First person may also make it more personal for readers by allowing them to associate even more closely with a featured customer in a title similar to theirs. Certain technical audiences like to hear directly from similar technical people. For an example of this format in action, visit Amdocs at www.amdocs.com. Some of the company's stories are in the feature-story format while others are in first person with head-shot photos of the customer.

The drawback of this format in B2B settings is the shorter potential shelf-life of a story that focuses on a person rather than the company. People change employers, and the featured organization may prefer that you discontinue use of a story that focuses on an individual's endorsement when that featured person leaves. But at that point you can possibly turn the story into a third-person account that has a few quotes from the departed individual, if your customer agrees.

If you choose to use a first-person story format for business audiences, it's advisable not to ask your customer to write the story. As with most story types, typically the most efficient approach is to interview the customer and write the story. Business customers are often too busy to write their own stories and are not professional writers. Plus, when you craft the story, you ensure that it includes and emphasizes the points that are most effective for your sales and marketing efforts.

Pros: This may be most effective when individuals or consumers are your audience, or for technology audiences that are very peer-to-peer oriented and tend to be distrustful of slick marketing pieces that come from the vendor company. This format works with both short or long stories.

Cons: There's potentially a shorter shelf-life when you focus on a person, who may leave the customer company.

Q & A

Question and Answer (Q&A) is another format you see used in journalism. Like a first-person account, it has a more personal feel and focuses on an individual. This may work most effectively with serious technology audiences that tend to be distrustful of anyone but their peers.

Atlassian (www.atlassian.com) does this particularly well in its customer stories. The company provides professional bug and issue-tracking software and enterprise wiki technology, targeting a very technical audience. On a Web site that heavily encourages collaboration and information-sharing between IT people, Atlassian has Q&A customer stories that start, "A Conversation with..." The company lists the questions asked, about a dozen, and the customer's answers. Most include snapshots taken of customers in their day-to-day work environments, including some in standard IT-wear—the t-shirt. It's a fairly simple, casual, and lower-maintenance format for presenting stories, but may not be as effective with some business audiences. Because this format publishes questions and then customers' answers basically verbatim, with perhaps a small amount of editing, less actual writing is required, which may lower production costs. But then you're somewhat limited to customers' actual comments, which may not be as organized or compelling as the paraphrasing and presentation of a professionally written story created after interviewing that same customer.

Pros: Lower production costs and faster story development since writing is limited.

Cons: You're constrained to the story the customer tells more than you would be if a writer creates a story from customers' interviews. To fully cover all questions and answers, you need more space on your Web site or in print.

Story-within-a-Story

When featuring your solutions at work in a customer's environment, it often reinforces the story to cite specific examples of ways customers put a product or service into action. One way is showing how your direct customer uses a product or service to improve its service delivery or offerings to one of its own customers. It's basically a mini customer story within the broader customer story, or "story-within-a-story."

Intellon Corporation (www.intellon.com) often weaves in such examples in its customer stories. The company makes HomePlug®-compatible integrated circuits for high-speed communications over a building's existing electrical wiring. The technology is relatively simple: power lines serve as the network backbone, turning every electrical outlet in a home or business instantly into a network access point. Many of Intellon's direct customers are technology integrators or original equipment manufacturers (OEM) who use Intellon chipsets to provide new services to their customers.

As an example, Intellon created a customer story featuring its client, Telkonet/MST NuVisions, a technology systems-application developer of powerline communications (PLC) solutions for commercial and government markets. The story discusses the reasons why the company was attracted to the technology and chose Intellon chipsets for its Telkonet iWire System. Then, the story provides a story-in-a-story on how Telkonet/MST NuVisions installed the iWire system at the Trump Tower, and Trump International Hotel and Tower, even including a quote from The Trump Organization.

The customer story inside another customer story seems a bit confusing, but can be a powerful way of showing the leapfrog benefits of solutions. Not only your customers are benefiting, but your customers' customers are too. A word of caution: This format can be more complex to produce. You may have the usual review/approval phase with your direct customer, as well as with the featured customer's customer. With the Intellon story, Telkonet/MST NuVisions already had an approved press release with the Trump information, so the company could leverage that information without additional approval. However, other customer stories like this usually require review by both organizations, increasing the time and challenges of securing approval.

Pros: Shows the domino-effect of a great product or service not just for your customer but for the customer's customer.

Cons: Introduces another level of approval, increasing approval time and the chance the story could be rejected. Requires more words and more space to tell the story-within-the-story.

The Customer-Focused Story

In a recent issue of *National Geographic* magazine, one ad stood out. The headline read: "Ameriprise Financial LifeDreams" atop a nearly full-page photo of a woman with a horse. At the bottom, it said: "Having a plan, and the courage to pursue it, helped one small-business owner realize her life's dream of establishing a sanctuary for injured performance horses..." When I turned the page, I fully expected a customer story about how Ameriprise Financial consulted with the woman to help her realize her dreams of creating the sanctuary, which would have been a typical customer story. Instead, I found a two-page spread, with photos, detailing the woman's life and the sanctuary's work—without any mention of involvement with Ameriprise Financial. At the end, the article encouraged readers to follow more of the story and see more photos on the *National Geographic* Web site, on pages "presented by Ameriprise Financial." What's most intriguing is a disclaimer at the bottom of the print ad indicating that the people portrayed are *not* clients of Ameriprise Financial. Effectively, the company is sponsoring a short feature story about a person and business because of the ideals that they represent, the same ideals that Ameriprise believes in: "having a plan and the courage to pursue it." It's a completely customer-focused story, just like a feature in a magazine.

You may not choose to feature non-customers in your communications, but you can apply this same concept with your successful customers—*without any mention of how you helped get them there.* But if produced with the same look and feel as your other marketing communications, or your logo is connected on a print ad, there's an implied understanding that your company was a part of the customer's success (Company X is a growing, profitable company and a client of ours). Sometimes that's all you need, especially when communicating with high-level decision makers. It just might be a format that some big-name customers would go for, especially if you are willing to foot the bill for a short feature advertorial in a relevant publication.

Pros: This format might work in getting high-profile customers to go on record since it's just a feature on the customer that does not actually reveal how you assisted the company.

Cons: There are no details about your relationship with the customer, just an implied understanding of a relationship or shared ideals.

Again, base your choice of format on what you feel will best accomplish the goal with your audience(s). However, if you plan to group stories on your Web site—always a good idea—then you should standardize your stories to a specific format.

The Expected Results Story

Sometimes an organization benefits from a customer story created at the outset of the relationship, before the customer has seen any real results. For example, a company that makes workforce management software needed to document its relationship with a well-known resort chain in order to sell a similar solution to other resorts. The customer had only used the software for a short time. The software company went ahead and created a story early to detail the reasons behind the customer's decision to purchase and how the customer anticipates it *will* benefit. The company plans to update the story six months to one year later for more measurable results. But creating an early version allows it to leverage the relationship and customer's name.

Pros: An organization has a story it can leverage quickly that covers the customer's selection process and expected results.

Cons: The story lacks hard results details, but you can project results.

Matching Story to Purpose

One of the fundamental objectives of any promotional writing is ensuring it meets the end goal. That means matching the content and format specifically to the audience and what you want the audience to do as a result of reading the story. "All too often people try to take one story and make it valuable at all stages because they're so rushed, but they end up creating a story that's not valuable at any stage of the sales cycle," says Steven Nicks, Partner and Co-founder of Phelon Group. "A story has to be for a specific audience speaking to a specific business problem, and more specifically needs to be written for a specific stage of the sales cycle."

Understand Your Audience

Start by thinking from your audience's perspective. What information do they want or need at different parts of the sales cycle to support their decisions? As they begin exploring products and services, they usually have some criteria in mind. For example, I researched e-commerce "shopping cart" solutions in order to sell information products on my Web site. As I began exploring solutions online, I had a general idea of what I wanted in terms of cost and functionality. I knew I wanted something that would integrate with my contact-management software and that I could easily change and manage myself on the back end. Looking at product descriptions and features on different Web sites, I narrowed down the list to a couple of options. From there, I wanted to know what experiences similar businesses—of my size and volume—have had with the software. Is it truly easy for a non-technical person to manage? I already knew what the software was capable of before reading the stories, but the stories gave me additional reassurance that the product functions as I hope and expect with other businesses like mine.

To understand your audience, talk with or survey prospects and customers. Make note of their top criteria and concerns in the selection process, and then build your stories from that perspective. Stories should answer the most common questions, concerns, and objections by showing success with other customers.

You also have to merge what the audience wants to know with what *you want* the audience to know. Perhaps a product or service offers features that a prospect doesn't even know she should be considering. I started my software search with some criteria in mind, but then the vendors themselves educated me about other considerations such as compatibility with merchant-services accounts (to take payments online) and security requirements. Strike a balance between answering prospects' questions and educating them about some of the key differentiators of your solutions.

Right Information, Right Time

Also analyze the types of decision makers involved in each purchase and how decisions are made. Different types of decision makers require certain information at each stage of the sales cycle. "A story created to move someone from awareness to interest is very different from content you create to move them from consideration to purchase," Nicks says. "Many content developers today don't have that view and don't think in those terms."

Perhaps a department manager begins a search and narrows down the list to a few vendors. The manager who will use the solution on a day-to-day basis, or interact with the vendor or service provider, has different concerns from executives. He wants to know factors such as how quickly staff will learn how to use the solution or how it works on a daily basis. The manager will recommend a specific solution that he likes best, and then pass those recommendations on to others for approval. Executives are most interested in the outcome of the expense. From a high-level view, will the company do business better as a result? How long will it take to recover the cost? For non-technical audiences such as this, provide layman's explanations on how the solution enhanced the company's business processes. Clearly call out details of results and how the product improved operations.

If you've identified IT managers as the decision-makers on your product at prospective companies, then your stories should include a fair amount of technical details. Those in IT roles will want to know specifics such as server and database needs, implementation time, integration with other applications, ease of administration, and ease of customizability.

If you're addressing both technical and business decision-makers in one story, strike a balance—give the tech specs IT managers need, but keep the story written clearly enough that anyone can understand it. You may need different types of customer stories to address the various decision makers at certain points in the sales cycle.

Story Length

A customer story can be anywhere from a few sentences to twenty pages. In a few sentences or one paragraph, you can tell a story that doesn't include much detail. This works best with electronic formats where you don't have much time or space for the information, such as commercials with Subway's Jared or online stories posted by Toyota drivers. Or, you can include very short customer stories in other marketing-communications materials, such as brochures. Usually, shorter stories work best with consumer audiences.

Story length depends, again, upon your audience, and where and how you plan to use the information.

If you're selling professional services to individuals/consumers such as financial-advisory services or life coaching, create longer stories— at least a few paragraphs. This calls for building more of a picture of the customer's needs and challenges in seeking services, discussion of how the professional assisted the customer, and then the outcome. That's hard to do in one paragraph.

Create longer stories for business audiences who need to understand, more extensively, how products and services work in a customer's environment, and exactly what results they might expect.

Choosing a Writer

Like penning white papers or crafting advertising copy, writing customer stories is a specific expertise. Writers need strong interviewing skills and the ability to construct an engaging story. It's more than stringing together a bunch of facts and quotes. And depending upon the subject matter, the writer may need an ability to grasp complex or technical concepts, and write about them in a way the audience can understand. Strong, effective customer stories require a writer who can collect and synthesize a lot of information, and create stories that have just the right level of content presented in a way that best educates and communicates the benefits to audiences. Here are some considerations for writers and those looking to hire them.

Just Writing or the Complete Process?

First, decide how much of the Seven-Step Customer-Story System process you want the writer to handle. At the very least, writers usually interview and write, and incorporate any requested edits from the vendor and customer companies—basically all parts related to gathering, using, and refining information. Many busy organizations prefer to hand off the complete customer-story process to the writer, from interviewing all the way to customer signoff. That gives customers a single point of contact for the entire process, and frees business owners, managers, marketing people, and others who are involved to focus on other responsibilities. It's advisable to first have someone at your organization pre-qualify customers as willing and able to participate. Then coordinate the phone interview with the customer and writer, or pass along the customer's information to the writer to follow up and schedule an interview.

Subject-Matter Expertise

It's a big world out there, with lots of different products and services. A writer likely doesn't need exact subject-matter expertise, but rather related experience. Strong writers are usually versatile regarding subject matter. However, if solutions are on the complex side, or have a lot of industry terminology, look for writers with proven abilities to write about complex subjects, even if they don't exactly match your subject matter. Complex topics are not exclusive to technology products and services. Insurance can be one of the most difficult topics for people to understand.

Even within the realm of complex/technical products and services, there are levels. If your customer stories are written for business decision-makers, then they will focus more on the business benefits. Stories targeted at information technology (IT) people will include more IT detail. Even then, you may not need to go into the bits and bytes behind the solution. The point is, customer stories are about a customer's experience and the benefits the customer has seen. Some technical companies are hesitant to hire writers without engineering or IT backgrounds, but you have to remember that you're creating a marketing/sales document—not detailed technical specifications or documentation. The writer doesn't need to know how to write software code to be able to write about the benefits of software. It's an important distinction for writers, business owners, and marketers to remember.

Writers don't need to have experience writing about your exact subject matter, but should have previous samples to show they can write in the style and level of complexity a project requires.

If the document sounds too stiff or technical, it will not be effective for its intended purpose. Just decide how technical your stories need to be, and find a writer with demonstrated experience writing for similarly complex subjects, even if it's not the identical topic. And as always, ensure she starts with a very thorough introduction to your solutions.

Writer Backgrounds

Many writers are versatile, so there's no real formula or specific background that makes a writer a sure fit or precluded from writing customer stories. Previous writing samples are your best indicator of capabilities. Customer stories most closely resemble journalistic articles, which depend upon storytelling skills. Writers with journalism or similar experience may be the closest fit. They know how to interview; write a strong lead, engaging headline, and subheads; use customer quotes effectively; and keep a story flowing from start to finish. Yet, those fresh off journalism positions may need a little time to get comfortable with the subjective nature of customer stories, and the fact that those interviewed have the chance to review, edit, and change the content. Rather than an unbiased journalism article, the story is angled toward the featured products and services, and collaborative among all parties.

Writers with marketing-communications or PR writing experience, particularly in content for newsletters and press releases, likewise possess those same journalism-style skills and are accustomed to this type of writing. Those with experience writing technical documentation (tech writers) will understand technical information, but may lack marketing-writing expertise. Again, go with past writing samples as your best indication of what a writer can do.

Social Skills

Writers will, in some capacity, interface with your happiest customers. It may just be on the interview, or it may be throughout the entire process to final story signoff. Anyone interfacing with your customers must be friendly, professional, accommodating, persistent, and patient.

"Friendly" means customers feel at ease during interviews and comfortable throughout the entire process.

"Professional" means being very clear with customers about dates, times, and logistics for interviews, and never missing a scheduled customer interview. Plus, extremely busy customers, who have graciously agreed to publicly endorse your solutions, may not patiently endure interruptions such as dogs or children in the background. It's fantastic that many writers can work from home these days, but conversations with customers should be protected from any type of distractions, whether in a home office or traditional office—especially since the writer may be recording the interview.

"Accommodating" means scheduling interviews when it's convenient for customers, taking into consideration their limitations in what they can discuss in customers stories, and collaborating with them during the editing phase to arrive at a mutually acceptable final story.

"Persistence" is required first during the interview. In the pursuit of measurable results, sometimes you have to push customers—politely—to encourage them to share information. Often it's just hard for them to put a finger on results. By asking questions that help them think about their status before-and-after the solution, and by being very specific with questioning, writers can often draw out this information. But it does take some persistence. The same goes for the approval process. Depending upon the number of parties approving a story, and what they have going on, it can take months. If the writer is handling this, he must check back routinely.

"Patience" also comes in handy during that aforementioned review phase when your customer story isn't at the very top of a customer's to-do list. And sometimes it's tough to nail down a customer interview time.

Writer Orientation

Writers need a very thorough introduction to the solutions that will be featured. Existing marketing-communications materials, customer stories, white papers, and product or service demos are all helpful, as are discussions with product managers, and marketing and sales managers. To write effectively about your organization, writers should understand the key value propositions, competitive differentiators, and typical objections that sales reps hear in the process. Give them a list of the top themes that you want to reinforce in your customer stories.

Writer Support

If you hire contract writers, assign an internal point person to assist them—one who is responsive and supportive. It seems obvious, but it isn't always the case. To do the job well, writers first need information: background on the customer's relationship with your organization, a clear understanding of which story angle will best accomplish your goals, and all the contact information for internal and customer contacts.

They also need internal feedback on the draft to ensure it's on the right track and reflects the company's key messages.

Writers need a go-to person when issues or questions arise in the process. Times have arisen, as a contract writer, when I had no real point person in a client organization because my main contact left the company. However, the company still wanted me to manage its stories. Inevitably, an issue or question would arise during the process where I would need an answer from a company contact, not just for my own knowledge, but also to answer a question from the customer with whom I was interfacing. If the writer doesn't have someone to contact when issues come up, it can end up making the vendor company look disorganized. Ditto when the writer has the draft ready and there's no one internally to review it, or the only person available doesn't read it for two months. Again, to the customer, it appears as if the vendor doesn't have its stuff together.

Finally, the internal point person also has greater authority to prod her colleagues when they are unresponsive to the writer, as well as reinforce the importance of the story to all those involved. If you are that point person, check in with writers working on stories, make sure they have what they need, and let them know you are available if any issues arise. If you are out of the office for any reason, have a back-up contact for contract writers. It makes a difference in the quality of your stories to maintain strong, clear communications with your contractors.

The Writing Process

Every writer has her own proven practices for crafting a compelling story from raw information. Regardless of how a writer approaches the story, it's essential to keep a few considerations in mind:

Angle

A story is all about the angle. The angle is what differentiates a story, making each one sound different from the next. The most valuable angle for your marketing, sales, and PR efforts may vary for each story. Before customer interviews, you likely had some themes in mind. After collecting information about the customer from various sources, determine the best angle for the story's intended purpose. It's often valuable for writers and marketing teams to discuss this after the interview and before writing begins. Perhaps you need a story that shows how the solution helps clients meet regulatory requirements more than a story that focuses on increased team efficiency. A story can mention multiple benefits, but you have to choose what the primary angle will be, and put that front and center. What main idea do you want readers to take away? That benefit will likely be featured in the story's headline and emphasized throughout.

Organize

Writing is largely an exercise in organization. First, organize all the information you've collected from customers and other sources. Then outline what you'll include and in what order. Before I begin writing, I group the raw content I have in sections: details about the customer in general; the customer's needs and challenges related to the solution; details about the product or service delivery; and then sections of benefits and results. Don't feel as though you have to get every single word or thought into the story. Choose what themes best meet the goal, and leave out minor points that don't add to the story.

Introduction of the Featured Customer

Early in the customer story, introduce the featured customer in some way. As discussed earlier, in a traditional format you might have an entire section or paragraph devoted to information about the customer. For other formats, weave in customer information to orient the reader regarding the organization or person.

The 'Challenge' Section

Devote some time to the customer's needs in regard to the products and services. Provide detail about why the customer required a better solution and describe the "pains" or problems associated with the customer's previous arrangement. Show the business impact of not having a better solution, while being careful not to paint the customer in an unfavorable light. If you have a strong quote from the customer regarding its challenges, include that as a way of emphasizing the customer's needs.

The 'Solution' Section

Describe the customer's reasons behind choosing the products or services. Other organizations find it valuable to know the thought-processes that others went through in selecting solutions. If available, include a powerful quote about why the solutions were the best option for the customer.

Next, briefly describe the featured products for readers. Even if readers know about the product or service from other marketing materials, remind them again in this context. If relevant, highlight how your organization assisted the customer in implementing the solution or the ease of getting the solution up and running.

Then explain how the product or service works in the customer's environment—in which departments, for what types of needs, how often, etc.

The 'Benefits/Results' Section

Identify a few main benefits that the customer experiences with the solutions. Be sure to emphasize benefits and results, rather than features. If possible, include measurable results to indicate the level of impact on the business. Again, include quotes if the customer provided strong, relevant commentary.

The success story or case study should complete the thought by showing how the customer ultimately met its stated goals. Otherwise, the story doesn't come full circle and show readers that resolution.

The Lead

In journalism and PR writing, a story's introduction is called the "lead." It's the first sentence or paragraph that captures the reader's attention and begins to set the context for the story. Take time to think of an engaging lead. If you begin weak, readers may not be hooked enough to continue. Non-traditional story formats, where you don't just start out with a company description, allow you to create a more engaging lead. Here's an example of two ways to start the same story:

Traditional story lead:

Since 1991, XYZ Aerospace Manufacturing has manufactured aerospace parts for the commercial airline and defense industries. From major airline companies to boutique aircraft makers, XYZ creates the pieces that keep aircraft flying high.

Creative lead:

When Bob Smith took over XYZ Aerospace Manufacturing in January 2001, ninety percent of the business's client base consisted of commercial airline companies. Eight months later, the company faced the biggest challenge in its history: the 9/11 terrorist attacks, which put a significant strain on the airline industry, as well as XYZ.

The first lead is accurate, but doesn't draw you in and intrigue you enough to learn more. The second paints the story in more human terms. How did this business overcome this major challenge? We want to know. From the first sentence, you are telling a story.

Key Value Propositions

After interviews and information gathering, peruse customer information for examples and details that reinforce your key value propositions. Out of the top three-to-five value propositions of the featured solution, which ones does this story hit? Ensure you weave them in. Also make sure you address some of the identified objections that customers typically have. If you can show that a customer had specific concerns during the decision process, and how the solution addressed those concerns, then the story will provide answers to audiences with similar questions.

Ending the Story

You can conclude a customer story in several ways:

Quote—A strong quote that underscores a primary benefit can provide a powerful ending to your story. Don't be afraid to end a customer story this way.

Wrap-up ending—You can also conclude the story by summarizing the main ideas for the reader in a wrap-up sentence or paragraph.

A **look-ahead section**—Many stories end by looking ahead to the customer's future plans. The customer may be planning to roll out the solution to other departments or locations, upgrading to a new version of software, or using the products or services more extensively in some way.

Readability

Just like any marketing-communications materials, customer stories must look inviting. A huge block of text without subheads or paragraph breaks turns readers off, even if subconsciously. It's a journalism trick to shorten paragraphs in order to improve readability, especially when the format displays text in narrow columns. Look at just about any magazine or newsletter, either printed or online, and you'll probably see short paragraphs of no more than two to three sentences each.

Headlines and Subheads

In any written marketing communications piece, headlines and subheads are the signposts for readers. They not only indicate what the story or a section will cover, but tell the story themselves. Don't miss out on the opportunity to reinforce the main points of the story, and your key messages, with heads and subheads. If you use those areas effectively, you convey the story's main points to readers—even if they don't read the complete story.

Be as specific as possible with headlines and subheads, while still keeping them succinct. Weave the most compelling benefit or measurable result into your headline. Example:

**Home Health-Care Franchise Reduces Costs by $35,000
Annually with Workforce Management Solution**

Or, you can create cutesy headlines that play off the subject matter or featured business:

**Help Desk Software: The Cure for Ailing Customer
Service at Children's Hospital**

Or

**PR Software Offers 20/20 View into PR Activities,
Results at Eye Association**

They're clever, but don't reinforce the importance or the real benefit of the solution. If you choose to feature a clever headline, consider including a subhead right under it that emphasizes a specific benefit, making it a "stacked headline:"

> Help Desk Software: The Cure for Ailing Customer
> Service at Children's Hospital
>
> *Service Team Cuts Issue Resolution Times in*
> *Half without Increasing Staff*

The top headline serves to garner attention while the second offers more specifics.

Subheads should be similarly specific. You may not always be able to name specific measurable benefits, but a subhead should emphasize some capability, benefit, or result:

> *Keeping Employee Insurance Premiums Steady*

or

> *High-Speed Access Installed in Each Hotel Room—in Minutes*

Quotes

Direct quotes add interest to stories and enhance their credibility. But it's important to use them in the right way, as points of emphasis or insight within the rest of the text. I've seen customer stories that are almost entirely customer quotes, with just a little bit of surrounding text for context. There, quotes lose their impact because they don't really stand out in the story. Other stories go too light on quotes. Of course, it depends on the strength of the information customers provide, but several (three to five) customer quotes are usually effective in supporting a typical two-page story.

In the journalism world, a direct quote is a direct quote—and is not to be changed. But in customer stories, where customers have the chance to review and approve their comments before they're publicized, quotes are more flexible. In the course of interviews, customers provide commentary, but there are "ums" and "ahs" and starts and restarts to sentences.

Customers usually appreciate it when you take their comments and make them more succinct and professional. It's also acceptable to link a couple of sentences together, even if they weren't said consecutively in the interview. If customers don't like their quotes as edited, they'll change them during review.

Editorial Style

Editorial style gives writers guidelines so that every story follows a consistent format, and matches all other marketing communications created by the organization. It dictates a number of considerations. For instance, should professional titles be lowercase or capitalized? Do we refer to the customer by his first name or last name each time? Is health care two words or one? Writers appreciate having a set of rules for these sorts of questions. There are established editorial guidelines such as *Associated Press* style, which many media outlets follow. Then there's Chicago Style used by many books, including this one.

Organizations often create their own stylebooks to guide marketing teams, writers, and designers on how to present information about their solutions, such as what names or terms have trademark or copyright symbols. Choose a style by which to standardize your marketing communications, whether it's a known style such as *Associated Press*, your own style, or a mix of the two. The point is to stay consistent throughout.

First Names or Last Names?

Usually, when a person is quoted in a story, the first reference introduces the person with the full name and title ("The widget has changed our lives," said Alice Larson, Director of Human Resources). In subsequent references, you would either refer to Alice by just her first name or just her last name. The decision depends on the context of the story. In most business communications, the last name is more appropriate. First-name references are usually more apt in stories with consumer audiences. These are generalizations. Decide what feels best for your audience.

On a First-Name Basis

Some customer stories only feature first names throughout. Sometimes it's because the stories lend themselves to that format, or to avoid revealing customers' full identities—or both. The Make-A-Wish Foundation's Wish Stories all refer to children by their first names. It feels right, not just because children are featured, but because the stories are more personal than business stories. Likewise, stories for consumer products like NutriSystem® or Crest Whitestrips® work very well with first-names only and protect the actual identities of their customers.

Stay Positive

In the Q&A format of customer interviews, customers often take the opportunity to offer suggestions for improvement or grievances about solutions. As discussed in the Intelligence Gathering chapter, that's valuable information to be passed along to relevant parties, but not to be included in the customer story. Keep the story positive and upbeat.

Don't Tell Them Everything

No doubt, there's a lot to say about your solutions. But a customer story isn't the venue for every single detail someone would ever want to know. Maybe you deliver consulting services in a five-step process in the customer's setting. Instead of outlining how you delivered the five-step process in every single customer story, describe your process in other marketing materials. In each story, focus on the customer's needs, highlights of the consulting experience, and the customer's results. The same goes for technical details. Explain exactly how a product works in accompanying data sheets and leave customer stories for real accounts of the solution in action. Otherwise, excess detail that's not directly about the customer takes a story off track and risks turning readers off.

Make Your Customer Look Good

Your customers may also want to present results numbers such that they don't call attention to a less-than-stellar previous situation. It's one thing to say that your customer had twenty regulatory violations per year prior to your products or services, and now has five regulatory violations. It sounds much better to say that the customer improved regulatory compliance by seventy-five percent, without mentioning how many violations the customer had previously. Being too specific about the customer's prior situation can make the organization look bad. Once you have before-and-after numbers, negotiate with customers regarding the best way to detail measurable results so that they are comfortable, but you also show solid benefits.

Presenting Measurable Results

If customers do provide specific before-and-after results numbers, you might try presenting them in different ways and deciding which has the bigger impact or will resonate most with readers. Let's look at a few (simple) story problems.

Example 1:

Previously, a customer spent ten hours every week manually creating reports. Now with new software, reporting only takes her about an hour, saving nine hours per week. In this example, you can either say that she saves nine hours a week, which is more than a full work day. Or, you can say that she reduced the time to create reports by ninety percent. In this case, saying that she saves more than one full work day seems more meaningful to readers.

Example 2:

A small business switches to a new health-insurance provider. Premiums for employees were one-hundred dollars per month before, and now they're sixty dollars. It seems more significant to say that employees saw a forty-percent reduction in their insurance premiums than to say they save forty dollars per month. Or, you could choose to present it as a savings of $480 per year. These are just different ways of presenting the same results numbers. When you have measurable results, consider the best way to present numbers for optimal impact with readers.

Localizing, or Localising, Stories

Companies that do business internationally often grapple with the question of whether to modify and translate customer stories for different audiences, to basically localize a story for the targeted geography. Sometimes it's advisable to alter a story for broader appeal, and other times better to stay local with your customer stories. You may need to decide on a case-by-case basis.

First, what about localizing the English in your customer story? There are subtle differences in how the United States uses English compared to other English-speaking areas such as the United Kingdom, Canada, Australia, and South Africa. It's "localize" versus "localise," and "center" versus "centre," to name a couple of differences.

Jonathan Kantor suggests sticking with American English. Kantor is principle of The Appum Group (www.whitepapercompany.com), a firm that specializes in the creation of professional business and technical white papers. Is this just "Americanist," or is there sound reasoning behind it? Kantor found the answer at EnglishPlus (http://englishplus.com/grammar/00000193.htm):

"Documents written with American standards of English in mind work for virtually all English, including that of the United Kingdom, Ireland, and the former and present British Commonwealth. American English is considered a universally accepted form of English, especially for business communications."

Kantor adds: "While a U.K. businessperson can fully understand a white paper written in American English, an American businessperson reading a white paper written in U.K. English will view the localized words as typographical errors. This decreases the credibility of the document for the U.S. audience."

So, if an American audience will see the customer story at all, stick with American English. However, if your story will *only* be used in places that follow Queen's English, in Europe for example, you may want to create it in Queen's English, which Europeans are accustomed to reading.

Look to your audience for their preferences. Try to provide stories that match their geography just as you create stories to match their industry, size, and other differentiators. That also goes for decisions about foreign translation. It's not worth translating a strong story from around the world if your audiences only resonate with examples from their country or region. If this is an issue, then try to create stories local to your various sales areas, or about companies with universal name recognition that will be credible anywhere. For example, a success story featuring the French office of Citigroup, a global name, can hold credibility when used in any region around the world.

Cater to Readers and Skimmers

There are two types of audiences: readers and skimmers. Some buyers will read every word of your story, while some will look to headlines, subheads, pull quotes, and sidebar summaries for the main ideas. Always write customer stories for both audiences. Build-in ways for skimmers to glean the main points of the story without reading it word-for-word. The headline is the number-one idea you want to reinforce, while subheads all support and add to that main idea, as does the pull quote (a quote that has been pulled out and enlarged in the final designed format). Summarize key points in sidebar, pullout content. What you choose to feature in a sidebar completely depends upon your organization's offerings. For example, you can include industry, location, number of employees, and then highlights of the customer's needs and results related to your solutions. If customers read nothing else, they know the customer is in their industry and what the business achieved.

In the written draft, highlight a featured quote to pull out, and the content you'd like to feature in a sidebar. That helps internal reviews, customer reviewers, and the designer understand how the story should look when complete.

Keep Stories Current

Once you capture a customer's experience in a story, the narrative may be effective for a number of years. But once your products and services change significantly, it becomes outdated. If a customer is on version two of your product, and you just released version seven, you might consider updating it. It's faster and cheaper than creating a whole story from scratch. In fact, updating out-of-date customer stories can be one of the easiest ways to generate fresh, relevant content. The customer was pleased before, and hopefully is even more pleased with the new features and capabilities you offer.

Find out from relevant account representatives about the customer's happiness level, and whether the contact person has changed. Schedule an interview to collect new details, update the story, and then get the customer's approval of the complete story again. I've seen companies update stories and create new press releases based on fresh information. The story is suddenly new again—as long as there's new information in the updated version.

Story Design

With customer-approved content in hand, team with a graphic designer for a professional-looking design format that maximizes readability. If you have a designer for all your other marketing-communications materials, it's usually best to work with the same one for your customer stories to ensure a consistent look.

Match other Communications

The question occasionally comes up, should customer stories look unbiased like a magazine feature, or should they match your marketing communications? If you look at customer stories produced by many *Fortune* 500 companies, those that have long been developing such marketing communications, the answer is clear: match your company's look and feel. Most prospects understand that a company develops such materials on its customer successes. If a decision maker has a stack of materials on her desk from a handful of vendors, all your information should follow the same look so it is easily identified as yours. Also, if you format your customer stories like something that ran in a magazine, then copies of actual articles that did run in the media lose their credibility and no longer stand out.

Always hire the best designer you can. Appearances really do matter in business. As a business owner, that's one thing I've learned. If you want prospects and customers to take you seriously, and read your materials, they have to look professional and inviting. Every time I redesigned my business cards and Web site, I noticed a corresponding increase in business. Investing in strong design almost always brings a return many times over. The best way to assess a designer is simply to look at past samples of her work and talk with her about her capabilities, pricing, and availability.

Layout

As with all graphic design, the layout should look attractive and inviting to the reader. In the written draft, suggest a quote or two to highlight in the layout ("pull quotes"), and content that should go in sidebar or overview sections. With that, the designer has the direction she needs to create a story that best showcases that information. Ideally, all the key pieces are located on the first page—a strong headline, a powerful pull quote, at-a-glance facts about the customer (size, location, industry, solutions used), and the results summarized in bullets. If someone only looks at this first page, they can glean the entire story. Then, the text fills in the details for readers.

Somewhere on the first page, preferably at the top, create a place to indicate which products or services are featured in the story. If you have multiple products and services, then marketing, PR, and sales people need a way to identify—quickly—what a story covers. It also helps your Web designer post stories in the correct places and categories on your Web site.

You may want to add the featured customer's logo as well. However, some companies have strict requirements regarding the use of their logos and may not be able to grant permission to use it in the story.

"About" Sections

Marketing communications materials often include "About" sections (usually one paragraph) at the end that describe the vendor company's products and services. In customer stories, I recommend this type of paragraph on the vendor company, but not on the featured customer. The story itself should have many of the details about the customer, so the "About" section would likely be repetitive. If anything, include the customer's Web site address somewhere on the story.

Stories that feature resellers/partners may also include a section about that company. Consider creating two versions of a story. One version can include the reseller/partner, so that the reseller has the story for its own marketing and sales efforts. Another version of the same story would leave off the detailed partner information so that all partners and internal sales reps can leverage the story.

Calls to Action

Marketing-communications rules state you should always have some call to action at the conclusion of anything prospects and customers will see. Customer stories usually have a fairly long shelf life, so you can't really add a call to action that can expire, such as a special offer. If you want to go beyond the typical blurb, "For more information, visit www...," then consider a couple of options:

More descriptive closings

For more information about how XYZ Solutions can help you reduce service costs, increase customer satisfaction, and improve cash flow, call...

An Offer

Schedule a free demo to learn how you can reduce service costs, increase customer satisfaction, and improve cash flow. Call...

Photos

Photos add a nice touch in customer stories. If they look good in the overall format, they help draw in readers. There are a couple of different ways to use photos in customer stories.

Stock photos

This can work well. Choose a stock photo that reflects either the customer's type of business, or what's happening in the story. A feature on a winery may show filled glasses on a table, or rows of wine bottles.

A story about a hospital would include images related to a health-care environment. If the story's about collaboration on a project, pick one of the many dynamic stock photos of people working together pro- ductively and happily.

Customers' physical locations

Photos of customers' actual office sites also set the scene, and if they are high quality, enhance the overall story. These might be profession-ally captured shots of interior or exterior scenes, or snapshots of proj-ects. Customers often have their own photos they can provide, either already on file or taken for the occasion. An ivy-league university supplied a professional photo of its tree-filled campus for a success story created by its longtime tree-care company, The Care of Trees. Sometimes images of the actual setup of equipment or hardware are of interest to customers.

You can ask customers to provide existing photos or take new ones, or you can hire a photographer, or take shots yourself on location. Whichever option you choose, make sure the photo is clear and well-composed so that it adds to the story rather than detracts from it.

Customer headshots

Customer headshots add an air of credibility to a story. Some customer contacts may already have professional headshots they can provide. If not, send out a photographer who's local to the customer to capture a shot of the contact. Some organizations run amateur (co-worker snapped) headshots in customer stories, which works in some cases but certainly not all. Atlassian, mentioned earlier in the chapter, uses a Q&A interview format to showcase each customer, along with shots of the interviewed contact. It's a smart move; technical audiences often respect other tech people more than slick marketing materials. Snapshots add an authentic feel. This also seems appropriate for the nonprofit, Kiva.org, which facilitates micro-lending for entrepreneurs in the developing world.

Stories that target business decision-makers, and use a professionally designed format, would look strange with a simple customer snapshot. It's clear the photo doesn't match the quality of the rest of the piece, and hence, takes away from the story's impact.

Print and Electronic Formats

Talk with your designer about how you plan to use your stories. If you expect to publish them only online, then the graphics don't need to be as high-resolution. The page count also isn't as critical. In electronic format, it's more acceptable for the story to run awkwardly into odd-numbered pages. Conversely, if sales reps are often printing stories for distribution, or you have them professionally printed, try to fit them nicely into one page, two pages, or even-numbered pages. Also, ensure the graphics are of a quality and design that supports printing. Talk with your designer about different printing options and the associated costs.

Find Story Examples Online

Find the customer stories and concepts discussed in this chapter at www.StoriesThatSellGuide.com.

As with any marketing-communications efforts, creating effective stories demands an understanding of your audience and their desire for information, merged with your own communications objectives. Find the format and amount of information that will best resonate with your audience, and provide it in a professional-looking format. A single story, captured in writing, can have a far-reaching impact.

Chapter Take-Aways

- Employ tried-and-true story technique with a setup/complication/ resolution flow.
- Determine whether success stories, case studies, or a combination is most effective, and choose the optimal format for your stories.
- Your audience's desire for certain information + your need to communicate certain messages = the optimal merging of information.
- Decide how much of the Seven-Step Customer-Story System you want your writer to handle.
- Always give internal and external writers access to the information and contacts they need to do their jobs, and be accessible to them during the process.

- Choose the most beneficial angle for every story.

- Ensure stories hit your key messages and competitive differentiators.

- Don't include *everything* everyone might ever want to know in your stories. Stay focused on the customer's experience.

- Write and design stories for both skimmers and readers.

- Keep stories updated.

- Story design should match other marketing communications materials.

8

Step 6:
Story Signoff

"Stories have power. They delight, enchant, touch, teach, recall, inspire, motivate, challenge. They help us understand. They imprint a picture on our minds."

— Janet Litherland, *Storytelling from the Bible*

A customer story isn't complete until the customer signs off. In a collaborative project with your most satisfied customers, where they are named publicly, customers should feel comfortable with how they are presented—and they ultimately have final say in what is published. They'll want to ensure that the story supports their own brand and messages.

Story Signoff is the sixth step in the Seven-Step Customer-Story System and a necessary part of Success-Story Marketing. Before finalizing a customer story, you have to ensure it meets your own internal goals and guidelines, as well as your customer's requirements. That may involve some negotiation on content and revisions, or regarding how the customer allows you to use the completed story. When a story gets stuck in the approval cycle, it's important to have some tactics in your back pocket to get it moving again. This chapter covers considerations, processes, and strategies to assist those managing the review and approval process with customers in the smoothest way possible.

Internal Review

Several parties are involved in the review of every customer story. At the very least, there should be at least one person at your organization and one at the customer organization involved in story review. When you have the first draft of your customer story, it should make the rounds in your organization first. Establish a regular team of one or two people who read every story that's produced to ensure the content includes consistent, relevant marketing messages, and follows company style. Usually, those internal reviewers are marketing or PR representatives, or business owners. In larger organizations, an attorney may want to review every story to ensure your bases are covered.

If other individuals close to the customer (such as account representatives or professional-services consultants) can add value or input to a specific story, then by all means include them in the review as well. But remember, the more people involved in the review process, the longer it takes to arrive at a clean, final draft for the customer to review.

Don't Delay

To save time, email the story to all on the "review team" at once and include a date by which you would like to receive their feedback. Check in if you haven't heard back from them by the appointed date. *It's very important to turn stories around to customers in a timely manner,* for a couple of reasons. First, customers often mirror your own level of urgency. If a story remains in your own internal review for weeks or months before going to the customer, then customers themselves don't perceive any need to expedite the process on their end. If you wanted the story quickly, then you would have delivered it to the customer faster—or at least that's what the customer perceives.

Secondly, circumstances change at customer organizations. Your main contact and customer story champion can leave. Companies may have had an unrelated bad-PR experience and decide to clamp down on customer stories. Or, something can occur that turns the customer's experience into less of a success. Get your stories to customers quickly to maximize the chances that they are still happy, willing, and enthusiastic about participating.

Types of Customer Approval

It's a litigious world, and many companies feel the need to get customer approval in writing. Over time, as contacts at your organization and customer organizations change, it can be valuable to have a record that someone, at some time in the past, gave permission to use the story publicly. Before circulating story drafts to customers, decide how your company should handle approval. What level of proof do you need? Is an email approval sufficient, or do you need a signed legal document? Every organization (or every organization's attorney) has its own comfort level on the matter. Here are the nuances of either:

Email Approval

Some organizations are comfortable with securing approval with an email. It's an informal approach that can expedite the process with customers. If your customer doesn't have to involve its legal department, then the process goes that much more smoothly and quickly. With this approach, customers would reply with an email with wording specifically requested by you.

An example: "ABC Manufacturing gives Company XYZ permission to use the attached customer story on its Web site, in newsletters, in sales opportunities, and for public-relations purposes."

But there are obvious drawbacks to this approach. You don't have a signed document indicating approval. Email approvals also don't typically get specific in terms of timeframes for usage, whether parts of the story can be used as stand-alone testimonials, and other details related to use of the content. However, email has withstood legal challenges. Consult your firm's attorney and determine your own comfort level. I have never seen a featured customer come back later and question or challenge the use of a customer story, but it could happen.

Pros: Faster, less-complicated customer approval.

Cons: Is not as air tight as a signed release form.

Signed Release Form

Many organizations featuring customers in success stories use a legal release form that customers sign. The release gets very specific about how the story might be used and for how long. When an authorized person at the customer organization has literally signed off on the story, companies have greater peace of mind in using the story publicly. But, presenting your customer with an official legal document often forces the story to go to the customer's attorney or legal department when it otherwise would not. Legal, of course, must give its blessing to any legally binding documents being signed by someone in the organization. Sometimes, owners, managers, or executives at customer organizations feel confident signing the release without involving legal counsel. At times, customer stories and their associated releases end up in an attorney's email inbox, where they may remain for weeks or months, or never emerge!

Customers' attorneys may also negotiate with you on the release's wording. Stay flexible and amenable to such requests, unless they are requests you just can't live with. You may need to negotiate a bit on certain terms of use, but most companies and customers can come to an agreeable solution.

Pros: The peace of mind of a solid, signed legal form covering every detail.

Cons: Potentially longer customer review and push-back from customers' legal reps.

Partner/Reseller Review

Before a story heads to the customer, determine whether any mentioned partners, resellers, or integrators need to review it first. Often, such parties not only sold the solution to the customer, but added some value in the form of migration, integration, configuration, customization, training, or other services. If you include more than just the partner's name and basic company description, you may want to bring the partner company into the review process to ensure all are comfortable with the content. Partners will want to make sure they and their roles in the project are properly represented.

SAMPLE CUSTOMER-STORY RELEASE

The following is an example release, and only an example. Consult your attorney regarding the most relevant wording for your own release form.

Purpose: This Success-Story Release is signed by an individual to provide consent to [Your Company Name] and its subsidiaries to use the individual's comments and the Success Story to promote certain [Your Company Name] products and/or services.

Authority: I have read the Success Story attached hereto, in which [Client's Name] is described, and I am authorized to execute this release on behalf of [Client's Name].

Release: Subject to the conditions below, [Client's Name] hereby grants to [Your Company Name] the right, without compensation, to (i) use, publish and copyright the Success Story, any results, findings or conclusions related to the Success Story, and the recorded, transcribed or edited comments made by me with respect to [Your Company Name] and/or its products and services and (ii) display [Client's Name]'s name, logo and other identifying information as part of the Success Story for endorsement, advertisement, and marketing of the products and/or services described in the Success Story in any and all manner and media throughout the world in perpetuity.

[Your Company Name] will not intentionally misrepresent or mis-state my comments, therefore, [Your Company Name] may edit my comments for space or clarity, or use my comments in whole or in part as it deems appropriate in its sole and absolute discretion and does not need to submit advertising or other materials to me and/or my organization for approval.

I and/or my organization agree that [Your Company Name] may exercise these rights by itself or through its resellers and other licensees who are authorized to market the products and/or services described in the Success Story.

Ownership: I and/or my organization acknowledge that [Your Company Name] owns the copyright to the Success Story.

Date: _____   Signature: _____

                        Printed Name: _____

                        Title: _____

                        Organization: _____

                        Address: _____

                        _____

Some companies also choose to create a release form that partners sign, indicating their approval of the story. It looks very similar to the one that customers receive but may include slightly altered language regarding how partners are authorized to use the story themselves.

Customer Review

Whether customer review goes smoothly largely depends on the groundwork you laid in Step 3, Securing Customer Permission. Way back in the customer-permission phase, you talked with customers, learned which contacts in the customer's organization need to review and approve your story, and listened to their requests and limitations regarding the story and its use. Unless you missed that step early on, review and approval typically go well.

Before circulating the story to customers, proof it one last time for any typos, and make sure you've accepted and cleared any edits showing in your document. You don't want to look sloppy in front of the customer. Email the clean draft of the story and the legal release form (if you choose to use one) to customer contacts. It's advisable to send the story as an editable document, rather than a PDF, so that customers can easily input their requested edits and comments right in the story. Otherwise, the writer or another person has to make those edits manually back in the original document, which leaves room for typos and errors. Here's a suggested text for story delivery:

Hi Joe,

Thanks so much for taking the time to talk with us recently about your experience with ABC Company products. We have completed and attached the draft of the success story for your review and approval. The story highlights ABC Company as a best-practices organization.

Please make any edits directly in the document and send it back. Also, sign and send back the release form. You can fax it to XXX-XXX-XXXX. I'll plan to follow up with you later this week. Let me know if you have any questions. We appreciate your time and participation.

Note that the email communication stays friendly and considerate of the customer's time and reinforces the benefit for the customer. At the same time you send the email, call the customer contact to let them know that you just sent the story for their review. Emails, with or without attachments, do not always reliably arrive, so always call as well.

Timeframes

If you need the story by a specific date, for a trade show or other event, let the customer know that you are eager to get it approved, if possible, by a certain date. However, customers have their own processes for circulating such things, and contacts are often busy, traveling, out sick, or on vacation. And your story is not usually at the top of their to-do lists. You can often do little to speed up their review, except to check in persistently and politely.

The customer's review time is probably the biggest unknown in the entire Seven-Step Customer-Story System. Your own internal processes and the writer's turnaround time are usually pretty standard. But you have less control over customers and their internal processes. I've seen story signoff take anywhere from an hour to a year. Even when you're dealing directly with the business owner or president of your customer's organization, it may take a while to get a response from busy people.

Revisions

Customer edits are usually minimal if the story has been written conscientiously. That means the story shows the customer in a positive light, stays true to what the customer said in the interview, reinforces the customer's own messaging, spells names and titles correctly, and includes accurate facts about the customer's organization. Typically, customers will make minor edits to their company information or their own quotes.

When customers send their edits back to you, review their changes. Most will probably look good. However, your customers are not likely experts in grammar and punctuation. At times, they may write something incorrectly, or even change proper grammar into poor grammar, thinking they are in fact correct.

Here's a common example: A company is a single entity, but many people refer to a business with the pronoun "they." In fact, correct grammar would have you refer to the company by "it." Countless times, customer reviewers have edited their stories by inserting "they" to refer to their organizations. In a case like this, you usually don't need to bring it up specifically with the customer. Customers appreciate someone who knows her grammar rules. Rather, make minor changes like this without calling attention to it.

If you counter with more substantial edits, send it back to the customer with revisions clearly showing so reviewers can focus in on them quickly. Also explain any edits that need clarification. Sometimes some negotiation on wording is required. Work collaboratively with the customer to arrive at a final draft that meets both your goals. Don't get hung up on a word or two, and keep it friendly at all times.

A Watered-Down Story?

It's a frustrating moment when a powerful customer story comes back with all the best parts stricken from the draft—a mere shell of the compelling story you originally sent over. The story you wrote may have all been true information—relayed to you directly by the customer—but seeing certain details in print can suddenly seem like too much information for customers. Or, your direct contact may have felt the content was fit for public consumption, but the department head, legal department, or corporate communications team disagree.

Often, those edits involve removing quantifiable-results numbers. If so, suggest presenting numbers in a more acceptable way. If you can't name a dollar amount, turn it into a percentage or another unit of measurement readers can understand, like man-hours reduced or number of full-time positions saved.

At other times, the customer may ask that you remove any mention of a specific benefit. For instance, the customer contact said that the solution or service helps secure its network more effectively. In the company's eyes, saying that implies that it did not have a very secure setup previously. One customer may have a problem with this type of detail, while others don't. When customers' edits take the punch out of your story, consider how important certain content is to your goals and plans for the story, and negotiate accordingly. Perhaps the editor at a targeted publication wants to see a specific theme that the customer prefers to remove. On the messages most important to your company, work with the customer to find a way to say what you need while still respecting the customer's wishes. Ultimately, there may not be room for discussion and you may have to settle for a less-powerful story. Customer happiness always takes precedence.

You may have to decide between (1) a less-detailed, compelling customer story that names your customer or (2) a more specific story that leaves out your customer's actual name. You have to weigh those two options with how you plan to use the story. Maybe the big name is more valuable than measurable results, or maybe your audience will resonate more with measurable results than the featured customer. Whoever manages the review and approval process with customers may want to confer with others in the company to ensure the best decision and approach for handling any issues that arise.

Final Signoff

With all edits complete and agreed upon, finalize the project with signoff from the customer. That means either a signed legal-release form, or an email with wording to the effect that the customer approves the story for your use.

Formally Thank Customers

When a customer participates in a story, the organization shares its time, opens up about its business practices, and publicly shows support for your products or services. Though the customer also benefits by receiving positive exposure, and by documenting results with a product or vendor, it's essential to thank the organization formally.

Always thank customers after they have gone through the customer-story process to ensure they feel valued for their time and input. It's important to establish a specific thank-you protocol, with an established point person, to ensure follow-through. Though email is now the primary mode of communication for most of us, it's too casual and easily missed among dozens or hundreds of other messages each day. At the risk of sounding like your mother, always respond with at least a written thank-you note. Thank-you notes make just as big an impression in business as they do to Aunt Martha. In fact, *Entrepreneur* magazine named thank-you notes as one of its "9 Tools for Building Customer Loyalty."[15]

IHS Inc. (www.ihs.com), a leading global provider of critical technical information, decision-support tools, and strategic services, does this exceptionally well. Though it's a large, publicly traded company serving some of the biggest companies in the world, IHS maintains a small-company feel in its customer relationships. Customers talk about their IHS account managers, sales representatives, and tech-support representatives as if they've been best buddies for years. That's because of each employee's focus on customers. It only makes sense that IHS carries that out in its customer-story process.

IHS hand-writes thank-you notes that are signed by every IHS employee and contractor involved in the customer-story project and delivers them to every person interviewed for a story. This happens even if the IHS team members are spread across multiple offices and states; the process just takes a little longer.

"We work in a small, niche industry, where most of our customers are on renewable subscriptions," explains Ann Bettencourt, U.S. Marketing Communications Manager at IHS. "We see them at trade shows and use their stories in a number of different ways. It's important that we treat folks right so they are left with a good impression. They're the star of the show in our case studies and print ads, so it's important that they're comfortable and that the process paves the way for multiple uses of their story."

For one recent case study, IHS interviewed seven people to show the use of a solution across an entire team. That means that IHS wrote seven thank-you notes for that one story. Two IHS team members and a case-study firm worked on the project—all three spread out across Texas, New Mexico, and Colorado. The team passed the seven thank-you notes among each other until all were signed. From there, IHS corporate in Englewood, Colorado sent out gifts—in this case nice IHS logo-branded 1GB pen drives—along with the notes. At the completion of success stories, IHS also sends customers copies of completed

---

15. Lyden, Sean M., "9 Tools for Building Customer Loyalty." www.entrepreneur.com.

stories in their final design. It's an approach that never fails to make an impression. In fact, after another recent customer story, the featured customer emailed everyone on the project thanking IHS for the gift and letting them know how much he enjoyed the process and appreciated receiving copies of his completed story.

After the process is complete, IHS also typically informs each customer when its story will be used in a new, public way, such as in a print ad in an industry magazine, to ensure customers are aware of public exposure.

Ways to Thank Customers

Hand-written note—Mail a handwritten thank-you note from those involved in the customer-story project.

A Call—Have the customer's account manager or sales rep place a follow-up call thanking them personally.

Logo-branded items—Send complementary company promotional items—a coffee mug, pen, baseball cap, t-shirt—along with a thank-you card.

Gifts—Send some other type of gift items, such as gourmet food products or a gift card for shopping or dining.

The framed story—Send the customer a printed copy of the story, maybe even framed. You'd be surprised how many stories end up on customers' walls, if the customer looks like a hero.

Access—If your CEO or another executive is passing through the customer's area, arrange a lunch between the parties. Or, invite customers to special VIP events you host.

Potential Roadblocks

Customer Changes

If you cleared your story with all the necessary reviewers before actually writing a word of it, then you should receive final approval with minimal hassle—unless something in the customer's organization changed during the process. It certainly happens. A customer company can go public or private, can be acquired, or may merge with another company. Or, one of the individuals who initially approved participation in the project may leave the company. You may need to get permission for the story all over again with new contacts. It's a frustrating process, but it's necessary and worthwhile in the end.

Find out who the new contacts are, explain what has happened so far, understand their concerns, and find a way to address those concerns while still getting a story that's viable for your sales and marketing efforts. If someone quoted in the story has left, ask if you can attribute those quotes to another contact. You may not be able to get approval, especially if the new contacts aren't familiar enough with your products or services to endorse them. If you provide a product or service that the customer company continues to use (as opposed to a one-time event or service delivery), consider letting the issue rest for a few months until the new contacts are also sold on your solutions and then approach them again about the story. You already have a draft started, so it could just be a matter of updating it.

The Black Hole

In my customer-story career, there have been a few times when a story went into what seemed like a black hole. Before starting, I had received customer permission for the project and then had great conversations with the contacts. Upon sending the story over for review and approval, I continued to follow up regularly with contacts. But even with regular emails and calls to the customer contacts, I wasn't getting status updates or any indication that the story was moving through the customers' channels. Or, the updates indicated the story was still on an executive's desk, or with legal or PR. After a while, the contacts would stop responding to calls and emails.

If this happens, consider trying some other measures to help get the story out of approval limbo:

Leverage relationships

Call in reinforcements! Find the person with the best, longest relationship with the customer contacts (if that person is different from the one handling the story process). Typically an account manager or reseller/partner, this individual may see or speak with the customer on a regular basis. Let him know where the story stands, and the recent update you received from the customer. When he speaks with his contacts next, he can bring up the story and probably get more insight on what's going on. He can reinforce the joint promotional, win-win benefits for the customer and agree on a plan for wrapping it up.

Take the burden off contacts

Often, customer contacts become the shepherds of a customer story in their own organizations. They review it first but then need to circulate it to other colleagues, executives, the legal team, or corporation communications—and follow up with those contacts. Your story is not a high priority for your customer contacts, even if you've expressed an urgency for it. If approval is dragging out, offer to take the responsibility off the hands of your direct contacts. Find out where the story is currently and who still needs to review it, and then be the direct contact with those parties. It takes the burden off customer contacts for managing the project internally, and gives you direct access to other approvers and any feedback they may have. Your contacts may decline the help. Some feel that because it features them and their department, that they should be the interface with others internally to ensure approval goes smoothly.

Send a thank-you gift early!

Here's a trick I've seen work more than once. If a story is stuck with a customer, and it's an important one to your organization, consider sending a hand-written thank-you note and possibly a small gift such as a company-branded item—before approval. In one project I worked on, a story had lingered with the headquarters of a major American fast-food chain for a couple of months. My client sent a t-shirt and baseball cap with its logo, with a card indicating that the company looks forward to completing the story and the joint promotional opportunities that will follow. The next day, the customer approved the story. Receiving a gift can inspire action. Think of it as the "kill 'em with kindness" approach. If you don't end up getting approval, at least one of your best customers knows you appreciate them!

The Customer Says No

There are rare occasions when a story goes all the way to the customer and then the customer declines approval for one reason or another. Hopefully, you've done everything you could early on and during approval to ensure it would be acceptable to the customer. But sometimes the sight of the story, and the customer's business practices or secrets in print, causes contacts to kill the project. If this happens, refer back to the "Alternatives to Public-Use Stories" section in Chapter Five.

Story approval is a critical part of your Success-Story Marketing efforts. Handle this part of the process smoothly with customers, frequently and patiently communicating until they sign off. If something happens during the process that changes the approval landscape, find ways to secure approval that are agreeable to you and your customer.

Chapter Take-Aways

- Circulate your story for internal review first.
- Include resellers/partners in the review and approval if stories talk about their contributions.
- Decide what's right for you: email approval or a legal-release form.
- Get stories in customers' hands quickly.
- Always call to ensure customers received the story by email.
- Negotiate and collaborate on customers' requested edits.
- Leverage contacts with the strongest relationships with a customer if the story is stuck in approval.
- Establish a formal thank-you protocol to show your appreciation after stories are approved.
- Remain polite and respectful of the customer's time and wishes regarding the story.

9

Step 7:
Leveraging Customer Stories

"Our species thinks in metaphors and learns through stories."

—Mary Catherine Bateson

When you invest in capturing a customer's story in writing, you can use that rich content throughout your sales, marketing, and PR. Whether your audience is customers, partners, employees, members, the media, investors, or donors, demonstrating your success and results increases credibility in your organization, products, and services—making all your promotional efforts more successful.

Leveraging Customer Stories is the seventh and last step in the Seven-Step Customer-Story System. This chapter, with five sub-chapters, highlights myriad ways to get the maximum investment out of your Success-Story Marketing efforts:

Building a Brand
- Advertising
- Campaigns

Marketing Communications
- Web sites
- Online customer communities
- Other online opportunities
- Newsletters
- Events
- Direct marketing

Selling with Stories

- Training new sales reps
- Examples in PowerPoint presentations
- Sales letters
- Email
- Voice mail
- Sales conversations
- Proposals
- Case-study booklets
- Up-selling, cross-selling with existing accounts
- An alternative to live reference calls
- Venture capital proposals/presentations

Spinning Success Stories into Media Coverage

- Press releases
- Pitching stories to the media
- Contributed articles
- Industry awards submissions

Telling Tales to Further Causes

- Employee/volunteer orientation
- Web site
- Fundraising appeals
- Grant proposals
- Newsletters/magazines
- Annual reports
- Advertising/public-service announcements
- Speeches and meetings
- Your physical environment
- Your hold message
- Public relations

Building a Brand

"Increasingly, customers are associating brand not with a message but with their entire experience surrounding the product or service. In other words, branding is now more about what you do than what you say."

—Bryan Eisenberg, *"Waiting for Your Cat to Bark?: Persuading Customers When They Ignore Marketing"*

"Branding" is one of those marketing terms we hear a lot that many of us couldn't explain if asked. Yet, we all seem to know what a brand is. Crest is a toothpaste brand. Coca-Cola is a drink brand. And BMW is an auto brand. But defining it or knowing how to achieve it aren't as clear. Officially, the Dictionary of Business and Management defines a brand as: "a name, sign or symbol used to identify items or services of the seller(s) and to differentiate them from goods of competitors."

For a clearer explanation, I turned to The Brand Ascension Group (www.brandascension.com), a consulting, training, and design firm that helps organizations build the perceptions of their brands. Suzanne Tulien, Principal and Co-founder, described a brand as "simply a perception that lives in the minds of your employees and customers and is defined by their experiences with you, your products, or services."

She further explained the physiological/psychological dynamics of branding. We take in information through our senses. Those senses create emotion around what we experience. And a brand perception is based on that emotion. From there, we make our decisions on those emotions. How we perceive a brand can be direct (from our own experience), or indirect (from someone else's experience recounted to us). That's where customer stories come in.

Stories about other people experiencing a brand, whether it's for a pain reliever or a $100,000 technology solution, reinforce the brand messages you're trying to convey. "If I've never experienced the brand before, the story gives arms and legs to that emotion and a succinct situational appraisal of the experience of that previous customer. I'm more likely to try the brand if I know others have and have been successful," Tulien adds.

You can reinforce your brand perceptions using customer stories in just about any sales, marketing, advertising, or PR efforts. Ideally, your messages are repeated throughout all your communications.

Putting Wheels on a Brand Message

I was a victim of all these dynamics when choosing a new mountain bike. For years, I've watched the *Tour de France* on TV every summer. With its usual highs and lows—daily wins, mountain challenges, crashes, and doping scandals—it's a very emotional experience as I root for my favorite riders. For eight of the past nine years, the winner of the tour has ridden a TREK brand road bike. In my mind, I connect TREK brand bikes with the stories of the winners of the most prestigious bike race in the world—for me creating a brand message of quality.

When it came time to buy a new bike, I went online to learn more. The brand has a line of bikes specifically built to be more comfortable for women of all levels. Looking at customer postings online, across various non-brand-specific bike sites, I found reviews of TREK mountain bikes written by real women saying it was the first time they felt comfortable on a bike. Finally, a salesman at the local bike shop (likely also influenced by branding!) said that TREK does women's bikes better than anyone else. First, the high-profile *Tour de France* association created an emotional tie for me. Then, the everyday-woman stories and the salesman's statement gave me further third-party validation. That did it. I *had* to have a TREK, even if it meant driving an hour away to find the right size and model.

Connecting Stories to Brands

With any use of customer stories, it's critical to ensure that the story's messages reinforce your brand. Start by making sure you've clearly defined the brand attributes you want to bring out in your customer stories. For example, if the ability to customize your software easily is a major differentiator for your company, give examples across multiple stories of how easy it was for customers. Or, perhaps your key messages are product performance, reliability, or return on investment.

For many companies, customer service is the brand differentiator. While each customer story may highlight unique themes or industries, you should weave your key brand messages consistently across all stories.

Those creating your customer stories, whether employees or external contractors, should have a clear understanding of your messaging goals. Make sure you talk with them before beginning interviews to ensure they are aware of these points, and that they ask questions designed to help draw out each customer's experience related to your brand. If your current marketing and sales materials accurately reflect your branding, then have writers study those materials as well. When actually creating stories, emphasize those core brand messages in headlines, subheads, sidebar summaries, and in the text itself. By doing so, you ensure that your customer stories amplify your critical brand messages.

Be Consistent

Brand impressions are built through consistency of your messaging. ITT Technical Institute (www.itt-tech.edu), a leading private-college system focused on technology-oriented programs of study, has conducted an ongoing branding campaign featuring its students. Its television and radio ads highlight current and former students talking about their experiences with the school and their career success after graduating. The ads don't focus on features such as the types of classes ITT offers, but rather on students' positive experiences. Likewise, the school's Web site includes student stories and photos.

Across all stories, the same brand themes appear: highly marketable career skills, career success, and work/life/family balance. Over time and multiple impressions, these stories very effectively paint a picture of what it means to be an ITT student or graduate, and build value for the school's programs.

Reinforce across all Communications

In the business world, brand associations are built the same way: continuous reinforcement of messages across *all* communications. Sage Software (www.sagesoftware.com) is perhaps one of the best examples of this. In 2006, Sage Software set out to increase awareness about its software and services in North America. As a subsidiary of The Sage Group plc, a UK-based supplier of accounting and business-management software solutions since 1981, the Sage Software brand was relatively new to the North American market. Over the prior eight years, the British parent company had purchased a number of well-known U.S. technology firms, including State of the Art, Peachtree Software, Best Software, and Timberline—all of which formed the new U.S.-based Sage Software.

Sage Software needed to build its own name and brand. Dennis Frahmann, Executive Vice President of Marketing for Sage Software's Business Management Division, explains the challenge: "Sage is a well-known brand in the UK and Europe, and even though the U.S. is a major market of the company, it wasn't very well known because we introduced it a few years ago. To build the brand, we felt we needed to take our advertising in a different direction."

The company engaged Dentsu America, the advertising firm for major companies like Canon U.S.A. and Toyota Motor North America. The firm created a campaign that capitalized on Sage Software's 2.8 million small- to mid-sized business customers. Called "Sage 360," the approach aimed to convey that Sage Software *surrounds* its customers with solutions (www.sage360.com).

Choosing the Campaign's 'Heroes'

Unlike most advertising campaigns, Sage Software chose to use actual customers, instead of actors, to reinforce its message. "Once we decided on the 360-degree format, there was no question in our minds that we had to use our real customers in their real work settings," Frahmann says. To execute the creative elements, photographers were sent to customer sites to capture 360-degree photos of business owners or managers in their offices. While customer success stories and testimonials have always been part of Sage Software's marketing mix, two things changed for the Sage 360 campaign: the concept that the company surrounds customers with solutions, and the idea of using customers as the primary way of presenting that.

When the marketing team thought about which customers to make the "heroes" of the campaign, it chose businesses for their stories rather than for their names–though Sage Software could easily have found some household names among its customer base. True to Sage Software's focus on small and mid-sized customers, the Sage 360 campaign features businesses most of us have never heard of, but which represent Sage Software's target market. Rather than emphasize products, the campaign focuses on Sage Software's broad portfolio, helping build the brand messages rather than individual products.

One campaign, featuring Cumberland Valley Vet, truly provides a 360-degree look at a busy veterinary office–with no less than six dogs, two cats, a parrot, seven staff members, and eleven human customers featured in the photo. It's a hectic ad, but that's the point. It's a busy office dedicated to animal care, and it's better able to focus on that mission because of Sage Software's accounting software, Peachtree. "Sage Software helps Cumberland Valley Vet look at finances from every possible angle," the ad begins, with the office's actual accountant featured prominently, a kitten in her arms.

Employees, Resellers, and Customers on Board

Early internal tests of the campaign concept "caught on like wildfire." Employees began contributing ideas about how Sage Software could leverage the campaign. Even the company's base of about 1,000 resellers and independent business partners were energized. On top of that, customers were excited to be featured, helping Sage Software build a long waiting list of companies wanting to participate. They knew the campaign would run in places such as the *Wall Street Journal*–an exciting promotional opportunity for these small- to mid-sized businesses.

Sage 360 began with ads in national publications such as the *Wall Street Journal, Inc.* and *Entrepreneur,* and niche trade publications like *Accounting Technology, HR Magazine,* and *Healthcare Informatics.* The half-page spreads, running across the bottom half of two magazine pages, capture readers' attention with their unique format. It's an approach that allows for full appreciation of the 360-degree nature of the photos.

Sage Software further executed this campaign across every marketing-communications medium it uses, including direct marketing, trade-show displays, and online. The most successful medium, direct marketing, took the form of email and snail-mail campaigns, each featuring one of the Sage 360 customers (more about this in the Marketing section of this book). Sage Software also launched a Web site devoted to the campaign (www.sage360.com), where customer stories and videos highlighting customers' full stories appear.

All internal and external teams involved in marketing had specific guidelines for how to carry out the campaign. And the company's resellers requested success-story templates that they could customize with their own customer stories. That ensured that everyone, everywhere, executed the messages and images consistent with the brand.

Exceeding Expectations

By all accounts, the campaign was a hit. At the outset, the company identified its goals as building awareness and preference for the Sage brand. Before the campaign launched in November 2006, Sage Software conducted a brand-tracking study. It repeated the same study six months into the campaign's run. Total awareness of the brand increased by twenty percent over the six-month period, which Sage Software attributes to the campaign. "Likelihood to buy from Sage" also jumped significantly.

Studies conducted by publications running the ads also confirmed their popularity. Among readers who saw them, readership and interest ranked considerably higher than average for the magazines and against past Sage Software campaigns, suggesting to the company that "people do like reading about other people."

Based on Sage Software's benchmarks, defined as increasing brand awareness and likelihood to buy, the campaign accomplished its objectives. "We were overjoyed with the awareness numbers. We're definitely continuing the campaign and are very comfortable with the return on investment," Frahmann says.

As the examples above indicate, brand impressions are built over time with persistent, consistent, and pervasive communications. Most importantly, define your brand's characteristics, choose customers who can support those messages, interview in a way that draws those details out, and then feature those themes prominently in your stories. The following sub-chapters detail some of the many marketing-communications avenues in which you can use your customer stories.

Speak to Your Brand Attributes

Merging the power of its customer stories with a very visible, widespread, and attractive campaign, Sage Software accomplished its branding objectives. Any organization can achieve similar results. Clearly define your brand, identify and capture stories that speak to those brand attributes, and share those stories with all your internal and external audiences in as many ways as you can.

Sub-Chapter Take-Aways

- A brand is a perception in the minds of your employees and customers, and is defined by their experiences with you, your products, or services.

- A story of a customer's experience builds trust in and knowledge of a brand.

- Consistently execute your branding across all your marketing-communications materials, and ensure all partners/resellers have materials that also reinforce your brand.

- Define your brand's attributes and weave them consistently throughout every customer story.

- Orient writers to those key messages you want to feature.

- Emphasize brand messages in headlines, subheads, sidebar summaries, and the text of customer stories.

Marketing Communications

"WHERE DOES trust come from? This is what every marketer wants to know. Without trust, marketers know that there are no sales."

—Seth Godin, *Permission Marketing: Turning Strangers Into Friends And Friends Into Customers*

From your Web site to mailings to events, all your marketing messages should move your audience into deeper levels of trust and understanding of your solutions. And those messages are not just reserved for prospective customers. Don't forget to communicate your successes continuously with all your constituents and stakeholders, including employees, partners, the media, industry analysts, and current customers. Customer stories easily work into most marketing-communications media for nearly all audiences. This sub-chapter discusses the many ways to use customer stories in your marketing.

Web Sites

Increasingly, buyers research new products and services online, before ever talking to a company representative. Most often, a potential buyer types keywords into a search engine and gets a list of vendors. He then follows those search results to a variety of Web sites, which effectively become the first impression he has of an organization. When a simple search yields your company along with dozens of competitors, how do you differentiate your business and establish trust quickly?

Build rapport in the competitive online environment with the voice of the customer, which is significantly more credible and memorable than your own marketing messages.

Customer success stories are one of the most effective ways to draw in visitors, give them insight into what it's like to work with your business, and offer them a sense of what to expect. If customers see that others like them had positive results, they feel more confident in choosing your organization. "You need to speak to the audience and a case study is a way of doing that," says Rafael Zimberoff, CEO of Z-Firm, LLC (www.zfirm.com) of Seattle. "Testimonials and case studies are ways the audience feels like they're hearing from someone other than our marketing department."

Hit Every Audience

In fact, Z-Firm speaks to all of its audiences on its Web site. The company makes software that automates frequent business functions such as shipping, faxing, printing, emailing, credit-card processing, and printing from within popular back-office business software such as Microsoft Outlook, GoldMine, QuickBooks, or Peachtree, as well as with eBay and PayPal. Additionally, the shipping software works with UPS, FedEx, DHL, and United States Posted Service shipments. If you take all the different combinations of Z-Firm's software and shipping carriers, there are more than seventy different combinations, not to mention customized use—and Z-Firm creates a customer story for each specific combination. "I've always felt like success stories are a great way to make a sales pitch," Zimberoff says. "Your prospect is in a vertical business, say they are in segment A. Here's an existing customer in segment A that might help this prospect 'get the message'. It's kind of like having a virtual sales force." And that virtual sales force pulls its weight. The "Case Studies" link on the Z-Firm site ranks among the more-visited areas and the firm's case studies are popular downloads.

Design with the Customer in Mind

As with any Web-design planning, it's essential to think through your customer's self-driven education process. Visitors aren't necessarily looking specifically for customer stories; they're just looking for details about your products and services. Organize your site so that customer stories are prominent and available throughout a visitor's time on your site, allowing the customer to read them anytime.

Offer multiple avenues for site visitors to reach your customer stories, even starting right on the home page. If you have space available on your home page, consider teasing one particular story. LANDesk does this with a small photo relevant to a featured customer, and then related copy: "Can you securely manage your field-based and traveling laptops over the Internet. Gwinnett Hospital System can." The box then links right to the hospital case study. Vocus (www.vocus.com), maker of on-demand software for public-relations management, uses a full one-third of its home page to highlight a customer's photo and testimonial, with a link to "More Case Studies." Those images change to feature a different customer each time someone visits the site.

EMC (www.emc.com) has a "Customer Stories" link right on the main navigation bar on its home page. It makes sense considering that someone browsing the site might want to first see what types of companies EMC works with. From that link, you can search for a particular story by company name, products and services, or industry/business solutions. But if a site visitor goes right to solution or product information first, links on those pages called "Customer Examples" take them to relevant customer stories. Depending on how they research EMC solutions, site visitors have multiple ways to arrive at the same customer stories—when they're ready for them.

Don't make your site visitors—interested potential customers or supporters—hunt for your customer stories. Consider where site visitors might want to access customer stories, and give them doorways (links) at all those points. Some companies push their customer stories into isolated sections on their sites called something like "Downloads" or "Resources," rather than with product or service information, forcing site visitors to track down stories. Worse yet, sometimes they're so difficult to find that you have to perform a site search or look at the site map to find them. If nowhere else, include links to customer stories with the products and services the stories highlight.

Keep Cases Organized

Large companies such as Microsoft have hundreds of customer stories on their Web sites, making organization, or "story banking," essential. Even if you have just a few stories, the same rules apply. Site visitors must be able to find relevant stories quickly. That includes not just current and prospective customers, but also sales representatives, external partners, and members of the media looking for specific customer examples.

Simple search or narrowing capabilities like drop-down menus help visitors find the stories that interest them. Organize menus by various categories: featured company, product, general category of solution, industry, geography, business size, etc.

Free Access vs. Curtained Content

Many companies struggle with the question of whether to give away certain marketing content freely online or to ask site visitors to provide their names and contact information in exchange. When it comes to customer stories, there are valid reasons for either option. By letting prospective customers access your content anonymously, they can direct their own online research without interruption. Plus, a certain percentage of people simply will not choose to download a story if you require their personal information in exchange.

Yet, if you ask for a prospect's contact information, you can capture those hot leads in your database and start establishing a relationship and trust with them over time. If you choose to require this type of registration, Brian Carroll, CEO of InTouch and author of *Lead Generation for the Complex Sale,* recommends keeping required information to a minimum. "Set the threshold of the information you want to receive from someone as low as you possibly can," he says. "If you ask for a lot of information, they either don't fill out the form or they may lie. Case studies and success stories are valuable, but be judicious about what fields you require from people. We start simple with a name and email address. Gather more information as you use other content pieces. You could use the analogy of dating. A little bit of exchange of information develops comfort over time. People who are dating don't share horrific relationship stories or intimate personal details about themselves on the first date."

Carroll also cautions that many people input incorrect phone numbers when asked to provide them, or enter their personal email addresses. Companies often discount registrants with Yahoo or Hotmail addresses as invalid (maybe sneaky competitors?), however, they are likely valid contacts concerned about their main business accounts receiving spam emails. "Competitors, if they really want to, will get your information one way or another. That's not a reason to ignore the majority of people who aren't competitors, but want to avoid getting their corporate inbox full of irrelevant emails," Carroll says.

Search-Engine Optimization

These days, it's not enough for customer stories to be compelling. Like the rest of the content on your Web site, they've got to improve search-engine rankings. Search engines are extremely text-oriented, making written customer stories excellent pieces of content to include on your Web site.

Basic search-engine optimization rules say to include words and phrases in Web content that people may use to search for solutions like yours. If well written, customer stories should naturally support your marketing messages and will likely already include keywords related to your solutions. But it doesn't hurt to go through stories specifically to make sure they include keywords and phrases.

Chris Winfield, President of the Internet marketing and Web solutions firm 10e20 (www.10e20.com), stresses that links and descriptive title tags further improve your search-engine rankings. "Customer stories are really good at attracting links or making it easier for people to link to you," he says. By links, he means finding opportunities to publish URL links to customer stories at various places on the Web. For instance, maybe the featured customer or partner involved will include links on their Web site back to the story on your site. Or, if you send out a press release on the wire about your work with a particular customer, include a link to that case study. See if a trade or other membership organization of which you belong is interested in running a brief summary and link on their Web site or in their newsletter to a story on your site. Blogs and discussion forums may also include links to customer stories, if they are relevant to the audience. More links equal better search-engine rankings.

Above all, Winfield suggests specific title tags on stories for the greatest impact on search-engine rankings. When you visit any Web site page, the title tag is the description of the page listed at the top left. The top of 10e20's home page says, "social media marketing, search engine optimization, website design"—all keywords for what the firm provides. Too often, companies are not specific enough. "What I see a lot is, 'Success story: Company X' as the title tag. But if you can say, 'Successful ERP Integration for Company X by Company Z' then that helps bring you up for all those terms," Winfield says.

Also consider how to present your success stories on your Web site, either the full text on your site or as PDF files. If you print the full text, then search engines can readily read all that valuable content, helping optimize your search-engine results. If you choose PDF versions, you need to ensure that PDFs are created such that they are readable. It's best to talk with your Web designer or search-engine optimization firm regarding how to create PDFs with searchable text. But some tips include ensuring PDFs are created with text-based programs instead of image-based ones; optimizing the title tag with keywords; putting other Web links in PDFs; keeping file sizes small; and including keywords near the top of the PDF. Regardless of the format you choose, you might consider providing site visitors a short summary first, with highlights of the story and solutions featured, and then giving them the option of reading the full case.

Online Customer Communities

We all want to feel part of a community. For that reason, consumer and business-to-business companies alike are beginning to leverage customer/user/member communities to keep customers informed, and allow customers to interact with one another and their vendors. Customer stories can be a valuable part of educating current customers about fellow customers' experiences in an online customer community.

Leading automaker Toyota Motor Sales created a micro site (www.toyotaownersonline.com) to provide Toyota owners with resources they need to enhance the ownership experience, such as maintenance schedules, and dealer, parts, and service information. In 2005, Toyota added a "Stories from the Road" section to capture customer experiences—directly from customers. Customers contribute their stories (and their photos, if desired) that speak to Toyota brand messages such as reliability, safety, and fuel efficiency. A California commuter talks about crossing the 400,000-mile-mark in his fourteen-year-old Toyota Paseo that just won't quit. A couple from San Antonio reports that their Prius allows them to make fuel-efficient cross-country trips, enabling them to visit their grandchildren more often.

Based on the success of that main site, Toyota launched a Toyota Truck Nation site dedicated to owners' own accounts of their high-mileage truck experiences. At once, the sites give current owners a means of sharing that feedback with Toyota and other owners, as well as offer owners insight into other vehicle options. "The goal of the site isn't to push product, but it does have a halo effect," said Jennee Julius, Advertising and Promotions Manager for Dealer Operations. "People are happy with their vehicle and people tell other people they are happy with their vehicle. It probably means more to those owners than us saying it. It's also another way to thank people for being a member of the Toyota family. We get feedback from owners, and it provides a tool for owners to tell their stories to us and other owners. It helps us create a community."

If you choose to create an online customer community, consider adding customer stories to it, whether those are submitted by customers or created by your organization. They're not just for selling to new customers. Stories help reinforce that customers belong to a community of other customers, and educate current customers about new ways to use and benefit from your solutions. The more extensively customers understand and benefit from your solutions, the more likely they are to continue loyally buying.

Other Online Opportunities

The Web is a vast place with new marketing opportunities emerging all the time. Pay-per-click advertising has become a hot way to *pay* to get your name in front of search-engine searchers. Ads are typically around one-hundred characters, giving you very little space to say anything. From there, those interested take that link to a landing page with more information. Winfield of 10e20.com suggests including links to related customer stories on landing pages. "Instead of overtly selling, say 'Learn how this worked for company X,'" he says.

Social media sites such as forums and weblogs (blogs) offer another opportunity to raise awareness about your customer stories online—if done in the correct way. While social media often become grounds for complaints more than success stories, they also serve an educational purpose. People participate in social media to share information and stay abreast of certain topics, and many of them may be looking for a solution like yours. However, you can't be overtly commercial.

General business sites such as Yahoo Answers (http://answers.yahoo.com) or Startup Nation (www.startupnation.com) cover a broad range of business-related topics. But thousands of more narrow topical forums exist for you to follow. If you serve the health-care industry, for example, find forums specific to the challenges health-care organizations face. Keep up with forum discussions as they happen. First, that gives you an understanding of your audience. Second, you might recognize opportunities to provide helpful answers. Over time and increased postings, you become a trusted advisor or thought leader. When appropriate, summarize a customer example in a posting, or drop in a link to a customer story to indicate how a similar company solved a problem. Pay attention to forum rules. Most prohibit explicit promotional postings, but if you're genuinely helpful, then you probably won't cross that line.

Blogs are another opportunity to share customer successes online. If your organization has its own blog, and a customer story fits within the context of your blog's purpose and audience, share a customer anecdote. By their nature, blogs are informal modes of communication, so stay conversational and relatively brief in recounting a success story. In other words, it may not be appropriate to include a fully written customer story in your blog, but you can provide highlights and then link to the full story.

Newsletters

Newsletters, either emailed or mailed, keep you in touch with all your audiences, including current customers, prospects, partners/resellers, and employees. You want to keep all these groups excited and convinced about your capabilities, especially as you improve and change products and services, and grow the business. Keep them informed so they feel part of that success. Customer success stories fit nicely in newsletters for any of these audiences. In email newsletters, where readers are less patient with scrolling down an email, include summaries that link to full versions back on your Web site.

Prospect Newsletters

Prospective customers typically sign up for permission-based communications such as newsletters in order to learn more about solutions and topics of interest to them. Secondarily, they expect to learn more about your organization in the process. Your goal: Build the prospect's trust over time and their perception of you as a leader in your industry. Highlight at least one customer story in every newsletter. Show a variety of stories to showcase your different vertical markets and types of solutions. That gives them bite-size bits of credibility, education, and validation of your products and services.

Regularly include customer stories in newsletters to your various audiences to educate them over time about your solutions in action.

Customer Newsletters

Don't forget to include customer stories in newsletters to current customers. They have their own personal experiences of your organization already, however, there may be other products or services they have yet to try, or other ways customers use solutions in best-practices ways. Sharing those ideas with customers helps them use your solutions more effectively, continuously reinforcing your value in their eyes.

"Our customer case studies reinforce to our existing users that they are members of a community, not just isolated users," says Zimberoff of Z-Firm. "They reinforce that other kinds of businesses or similar businesses use the same solution, and that again helps confirm in the customer's mind that they did the right thing. It's a tool to inform the entire community."

Partner Newsletters

Run customer stories in communications to partners/resellers to keep them updated on the types of customers using your solutions and in what ways. That helps all partners pick up new ideas about ways to bring solutions to their customers. Plus, they become aware of the types of stories available to support their own sales efforts.

Employee Newsletters

From accounting to HR to customer service, everyone in your organization needs to understand how your products or services help customers—especially those with minimal direct interaction with customers. They don't have the chance to hear those first-hand stories and know the impact the organization has on its customers. It's not only educational for them—knowing who and how solutions are used—but inspirational. They know that, even though they may not serve customers directly, they work for an organization that makes a difference, boosting their morale and motivation. "As we grow, it's hard to keep employees informed about the breadth of things we're doing across the company, so we use customer stories as internal educational tools as well," says Donita Prakash of Acumen Solutions.

Events

At live events, attendees expect to be both entertained and educated. They're looking for insight on how others meet business challenges effectively. Stories capture their attention and are more memorable than just about any other form of information delivery. Events offer a number of ways to share customer stories with all your audiences, including prospects, current customers, partners/resellers, and the media.

Live Presentations

Workforce-management solutions provider Kronos® Incorporated (www.kronos.com) brings together about 1,500 workforce management professionals for its annual KronosWorks conference. Current customers, prospects, and partners look forward to the event's highlight, the company's Best Practices Awards Program. As part of that, award-winning customers present details about their best-practices uses of Kronos solutions. According to Michele Glorie, Senior Director, Corporate Communications, Kronos added those presentations based on feedback that attendees wanted to hear those stories.

Live examples presented by customers and partners give attendees concrete examples of how others benefit from products and services, and ideas for how to use existing solutions better or how new solutions might work in their environments. Likewise, many current customers and partners want the opportunity to showcase their innovation and results to their peers. When selecting story presenters, as with any approach to customer stories, ensure speakers represent a wide range of customers and solutions to hit your various types of customers.

Customer stories—presented by customers, partners, or company representatives—also pack a punch in online "webinars," teleclasses, and smaller in-person events for prospects and customers. In promotional efforts before your event, mention the real customer examples that you'll feature, which will likely increase interest and participation. Prospects don't want to hear from just company representatives about your products and services. Rather, real customers bring a level of credibility only possible from peer-to-peer presentations.

Written Stories

Most of us have attended trade shows and picked up bags full of glossy marketing materials, most of which are expressed in the vendors' words. To stand out, you need to communicate with prospects in a way that resonates with them and their current challenges. In conversations with prospects at large events, mention a customer in a related business who has seen success with your solutions. Ideally, come with an assortment of different printed customer stories that represent your vertical industries, geographic areas, and different products and services. It's both impressive and powerful to share with a prospect the story of a customer facing and solving the same challenges.

Direct Marketing with Stories

Two seconds, maybe three. That's about all the time you have to convince someone to read your promotional email or snail mail. According to direct-mail stats, about ninety-eight to ninety-nine percent of the time, people hit delete or toss the item. To be read-worthy, your message must be clear and targeted specifically for the recipient. Customer stories are one tactic to get your direct marketing noticed.

Telling Small Tales

Direct marketing delivers promotional messages straight to potential customers on an individual basis–right to their mailboxes or email accounts. Again, here is another opportunity where a customer story can get readers to notice your communication and linger longer. If you apply the "like me" factor of stories to direct marketing, by featuring customers who are like recipients of your mailings, readers can more readily identify with the message and become intrigued to learn more about this person or organization facing and solving similar challenges.

But in direct marketing–a medium with a notoriously short attention span–telling stories requires restraint or you risk turning off the reader. We've all received direct-mail letters with stories, appeals, or product pitches that extend three or four pages. That is almost always too much, especially if you haven't built much of a relationship with the recipient. For instance, I'm more apt to read a long letter featuring a story from the Humane Society, of which I've been a member for years, because I know, like, and trust them already. But if I receive a three- or four-page letter from a national nonprofit I've never heard of, from halfway across the country, I'd see all the text and stop before even getting into the first paragraph. In direct marketing, less is often more. Get the reader's interest and then give him links or ways to explore further.

Snail Mail that Works

Design That Works (www.designthatworks.com), an Atlanta-based marketing and creative firm, does this so well that people have actually called with their address changes–to ensure they keep receiving the firm's mailings, which include postcards featuring satisfied customers. The firm's use of success stories began in the late '90s, when owner Linda McCulloch sought a way to differentiate Design That Works and show the value of its services to prospects. With a name like Design That Works, the firm wanted to show it works, but felt a little uncomfortable talking itself up. "The marketing communications business can be so full of smoke and mirrors, and you're always telling everyone how great you are," McCulloch says. "I don't like to blow my own horn excessively, so I felt that if I could get my clients to blow my horn for me that that would be more convincing to potential clients."

The customer "horn-blowing" began with the firm collecting testimonial letters from clients, eventually growing to a two-inch thick binder. But Design That Works wanted to take that rich success-story content beyond just sharing letters with prospects or running a few quotes on its Web site. The success-story postcard series was born. Though initially hesitant about asking customers to be featured in mass mailings, McCullough found they were thrilled to share their results–and to benefit from the exposure of being "stars" in the campaigns.

The 5½" x 8½" postcards feature specific client projects, with static copy about the firm running down the left-hand side. Three client-focused sections tell the story: The Challenge, The Result, The Quote (client testimonial), each about one paragraph. They also include small images of the project's output, such as a Web site screen shot, marketing collateral, or trade-show signage. Though it isn't much copy, it still tells a story of the client, its goals, and how the business achieved success (see a sample at www.StoriesThatSellGuide.com).

Each mailing, about three times a year, showcases a different client's challenges and results. The goal: stay top of mind with clients and prospects. And it's worked. The postcards stand out among all the mail clients and prospects receive, and show audiences the specific results that other companies have experienced with the help of Design That Works.

While the postcards are one of many marketing tactics Design That Works employs, the postcard is, at times, the piece that finally motivates folks to make a move. "I've gotten really good feedback on the post-cards over the years," McCulloch says. "They're to the point, easy to read, and colorful so people remember them. For what it costs to print and mail them, they're a great way of staying in front of people."

Continuously expanding the success-story concept, Design That Works ditched its traditional company brochure and replaced it with a success-stories booklet that pulls all the postcard content into one collateral piece. With nine client projects included, the booklet tells a complete story of the firm's capabilities and results. Likewise, McCulloch brings in client stories anecdotally in meetings with prospects. In one case, that got the decision-maker engaged and interested, turning into a sale. "There's nothing better than saying, 'Let me just tell you a story about how we helped a client differentiate themselves,'" she says.

Design That Works also encourages clients to use their own testimonials and success stories in telling their stories. "It works for just about any company if the story is compelling, has a ring of truth, and is spoken with passion," she adds.

A Winning Campaign

Success-story-based direct marketing has also worked exceptionally well for a large company campaign, Sage Software's "Sage 360" (www.sage360.com)–actually topping all other media used in the broadly executed campaign in terms of results. Dennis Frahmann, Executive Vice President of Marketing for the Business Management Division, attributes the results largely to the personalization of each direct-mail piece. However, the focus on real customers helps increase reader interest to look further at the materials.

The 360 campaign has a number of direct-marketing variations. It features customers on postcards, in emails, and in more elaborate direct-mail pieces. Each one highlights a different customer's success story. Postcards, 11? x 6 inches, capture the 360-degree customer photos on one side with brief summaries of the customer's experience with Sage Software on the other side. Sent to current customers, the postcards encourage them to learn more about other Sage Software solutions by attending one of several upcoming free live webcasts about the software. The email campaigns follow a similar approach. Each direct-marketing piece includes a personalized Web address, where customers can go online to learn more about the specific solutions that may be most applicable to them, based on Sage Software's existing knowledge of those customers. The high response rates come from that powerful combination of a featured customer, with an issue similar to one the recipient is facing, and an easy way for customers to learn more.

Tips for Direct-Mail Storytelling

Both companies—one small, one large—seem to be beating the direct-marketing odds and getting noticed by featuring real customers. Both used postcards, a highly effective option because readers don't have to decide whether to open it first. The images and messages are simply right there in front of them. But your direct marketing featuring customer stories can take a number of other forms: sales letters, flyers/self-mailers, article reprints on your company, articles on a topic of interest to the recipient, complete printed customer stories, white papers, newsletters, event invitations, and research reports. In any of these formats, you can weave in a customer story.

If you plan to integrate direct marketing featuring customer successes into your own efforts, keep in mind the following tips:

Clearly state customer results

Don't stop with just a customer testimonial, for testimonials don't tell a story. Help the reader empathize with and get to know the featured customer by briefly touching on his challenge, the solution that was applied, and then the benefits/results the featured customer has experienced. Use clear, easy-to-understand language, instead of industry jargon the reader might not understand.

Tailor for the audience

Just featuring a customer's story is not enough. The message must still match up with the recipient's demographic profile or his possible needs/challenges. Or, talk about a message or challenge that might be universally appealing to a broad swath of customers, such as an issue all small, growing businesses face.

Use graphics well

As with any marketing communications, don't let it go out the door without professional-looking design and copywriting. Perhaps use a customer photo, as Sage Software does. Among a stack of mail or the recipient's inbox, nice graphics, photos, and headlines increase your direct-mail open rate (the percentage of people who open the communication).

Include a call to action

Encourage readers to take some action now. That might be a special, limited offer; an invitation to an upcoming event or webinar; an encouragement to read the rest of the featured company's story online; or an offer of a free report that the prospect or customer can download from your Web site. Always give them some next step to take.

Follow email rules

If email is part of your direct marketing campaign, learn and follow spam rules. Find details on the guidelines in the *Direct Marketing Association's Guidelines for Ethical Business Practice* (www.the-dma.org/guidelines/EthicsGuidelines.pdf). Use the "Find" feature on your computer to search for the relevant terms such as "e-mail" and "online," as this topic is covered in several sections of the document.

For more information about direct-marketing best practices, visit the Direct Marketing Association at www.the-dma.org.

Clearly, direct marketing rooted in reality can help mailings stand out in the pile.

Customer stories add a compelling element to all your marketing communications. Just ensure that you have a broad range of stories so that a prospect can find one that sounds like his situation.

Sub-Chapter Take-Aways

- Don't force Web site visitors to hunt for customer stories. Offer multiple, logical doorways to the information.
- Consider teasing one story on your home page, and change it often.
- Organize stories by various categories on your Web site: featured company, product, solutions, industry, geography, products, business size, etc.
- If you require customers to register for stories, only ask for a small amount of information, such as name and email address.
- Optimize stories for search engines.
- Include stories in online customer communities.
- Feature customer examples in newsletters for prospects, customers, partners, and employees.
- Invite customers to present their live case studies at events, webinars, and teleclasses.
- Bring a wide range of stories to trade shows and pull out just the right one for each prospect.
- Set direct marketing apart with storytelling.

Selling with Stories

> *"Nobody has time to try anything anymore. Everyone wants to know before they buy something that it will succeed. And they need to have a high degree of confidence before they touch a product or service that it's going to meet their needs, and the customer story helps establish that."*
>
> —Rafael Zimberoff, CEO, Z-Firm, LLC

It doesn't matter if you're a one-person business, a nonprofit, or a multi-billion-dollar global corporation. In order to make a sale or gain support, you have to connect with people on an individual level. They have to like and trust you before selecting you. If they don't know your organization, or don't have a personal referral from someone they know, they need evidence that you're credible and can accomplish what you say you can.

By the time prospects get to the sales process, they have seen your marketing materials and perhaps talked with a sales rep–two very biased sources of information. Customer stories provide that third-party credibility so essential to removing risk in prospects' minds.

Jill Konrath, author of *Selling to Big Companies*, repeatedly reinforces the importance of real customer stories and results. She says that corporate decision makers "are especially interested in how similar companies have tackled the very same challenges they're facing."[16] It's a "like me" dynamic that's powerful in just about any marketing or sales opportunity.

This sub-chapter covers the many nuances of using customer stories in the sales process, from timing to type of content to ensure sales reps know how to use that powerful content.

---

16. Konrath, Jill, *Selling to Big Companies*

Timing Story Use

In sales and marketing circles, opinions vary widely about when to use customer stories in the process. Do you leverage them early for lead generation or opening doors? Or later as proof sources? In reality, those selling well use them throughout the *entire* sales process, as well as *before* the process even begins—as training tools for sales reps. Before interacting with prospects, the sales person has to understand the full value of what she is selling—the difference the solution makes for the customer. Then as you develop a relationship with potential customers, you start with tidbits of customer stories and build until you reveal the entire picture in complete detail. In the beginning, you may give the audience one piece of information or a hint of the broader story.

As prospects move through the sales process, they are exposed to increasingly more information to help them make the final decision, including detailed metrics and results.

Training Reps with Stories

Before selling anyone else on solutions, sales people must be sold first. If you don't believe in and understand the value of what you're selling, it's pretty hard to communicate it clearly, strongly, and convincingly to anyone else. Too many sales people lack that conviction in their own products, according to Konrath. "It's amazing to me how many sellers who have worked for their companies for a long time don't really understand the value they are bringing to the table," she says.

That's why it's important to include customer stories as part of the sales-training process. Doing so educates them about how the products or services are actually used by customers. What are the typical challenges a customer faces that require a new option? How do customers leverage the products or services in their daily workflow? Or, how does the typical project play out with a customer? What are typical benefits that customers experience?

Just as critical, customer stories get sales people excited and motivated about what they're selling. They have to be evangelists for these products and services or they can't effectively convert prospects to customers. In fact, that emotional connection is essential to sales success. "If sellers just feel like they're dialing for dollars, they don't stay at it very long, they abandon their account entry campaigns because they don't want to be a pest and they don't understand the true value," Konrath adds. "But if sales people are shown multiple customer stories and understand how their offering significantly impacts potential customers, they'll pursue accounts much longer and with a clear picture in their mind of how they can positively affect the prospect's business. It significantly shifts their own mindset. This is much more important than most people realize."

You can bring customer stories into sales training in multiple ways: orally tell some of your best stories to reps in training; include written stories in training binders; give reps video or audio interviews with customers; or do all of the above. The more stories reps hear, the more they will understand what they're selling and be able to recall those stories in the next step–talking with actual prospects.

Door Openers

Once they are fully educated and motivated themselves, sales people need those same customer stories to begin conversations with prospects. Most prospects are so busy and so bombarded with information that any effort to get their attention by phone, mail, email, or in person must stand out. It's important to have succinct customer-data points in your back pocket, such as time-savings, cost-savings, or other relevant measures of success for your product or service.

Most often, sales people begin communicating with a potential customer via voice mail–just the perfect venue for dropping a different data point with each successive contact. Here's how Konrath suggests bringing in one little piece of the customer story early in the process:

"Hi Bob, Jill Konrath calling. I'd like to talk with you about how to increase your sales conversion rate. One of our recent clients was able to increase conversions by sixty-two percent in a four-month period."

The next voice mail or interaction might go something like this:

"Hi Bob, Jill Konrath calling again. I mentioned last time I called that a client was able to increase its sales conversion rate. They also saw a significant impact on average order size. In fact, that went up four-teen percent in a three-month period."

Or, you can drop similar proof points in follow-up emails or letters to prospects. In this type of story use, you don't even need to name the customer you're referencing. What's most important here is the data to support the value proposition and begin getting the customer interested enough to consider changing his current situation.

However, if the referenced customer is in the same industry or is recognizable to the prospect, it might be beneficial to name-drop in that case. To that end, the more stories you have across all the different industries and types of organizations you serve, the better you are prepared to pull out just the right examples to mention to a prospect.

At this phase, some companies choose to use customer story-booklets as a key piece of collateral to share with prospects by mail or in person before more detailed conversations commence. The booklets highlight success stories, short overviews of customers' experiences, to give the prospect a broad idea of the types of customers you serve.

Education/Evaluation

Once you secure a conversation with a prospect, be ready with more examples and more details about other customers' experiences that are particularly relevant to the prospect.

As prospects move through the sales process, they begin their due diligence–some formal, some informal. Initially, they're looking for answers about how the products or services will work in their environments and with their people. Are services delivered on site? How long is a typical engagement? What are the upfront and ongoing costs? Do new solutions work with existing ones? Their goal: narrow down to a short list to consider further.

As a vendor, this is when you need to give buyers a really solid picture of what it would be like to work with you. As part of your sales toolkit, PowerPoint presentation, or your sales proposal, customer stories help buyers answer these questions. Stories provide the next level of detail buyers need to decide to move forward or not. At the same time, success stories reinforce your credibility and value in the mind of the prospect by showing them that you have happy customers—hopefully just like them—who have seen success with your solutions.

"For a lot of people, there's the typical fear, uncertainty and doubt," says Brian Carroll, CEO of InTouch and author of *Lead Generation for the Complex Sale.* "'Are you any good? Do you understand me?' As buyers start to look at vendors and who you've worked with, they want to know, 'Have you worked with someone like me?' As you're getting to the point where people are asking those questions, that's where the success stories are really pivotal to prove that. If sales people don't have tools like customer stories in the mid to late stages of the buying process, they aren't on fair footing because customers need to see—especially if you sell something intangible like services—what the solution looks like."

Remember that each company and prospect is different. While there might be common concerns and questions, individual concerns vary. For example, if a prospect had a bad experience with its previous vendor's customer service, then service may be the prospect's number-one concern. Share a customer story that includes mention of another customer's service experience. Or, a company that provides health-insurance plans for small businesses needs to reinforce to busy Human Resources teams that administering the health plans won't add to their many responsibilities—that, in fact, going with the insurance company will ease the burdens on the HR team. It's each sales person's job to listen for those concerns, and respond with the appropriate customer stories to answer objections. In this phase, leverage written success stories or case studies, or video or audio content.

Validation

When the prospect has narrowed the short list to one or two providers, it's time to go about the process of validating the proposed solution. The amount of proof a prospect needs usually depends upon the size of the investment up for consideration and the perceived risks of the decision, such as short-term disruption and time involved. At this stage, many prospects want detailed accounts of other customers' return on investment (ROI) results or payback period, the time required to recoup the costs of the solution. Managers need this hard data in order to make the sale internally to executive decision-makers at the organization. Ensure prospects are equipped with the right evidence to help make the sale.

The proof points vary depending on what you provide. They don't always have to be translated to hard numbers, though some prospects will want that kind of quantification. For a nonprofit providing constructive summer and after-school programs for girls, the metrics might be that grades went up and behavioral problems went down for a girl that participated in its programs. An organizational-development consulting firm would want to show how its services increased employee satisfaction and lowered turnover. The best approach is to understand your prospects and what proof points they want, and work on capturing them in your stories.

Up-Selling and Cross-Selling

Don't miss out on the opportunity to leverage customer stories with existing customers. Up-sell more of your products and services to customers by using examples from similar customers. It's also extremely effective to capture a story on a subset of an organization —one division, department, location, or franchisee—and then take that story to other divisions, departments, locations, and franchisees within the same organization. There's added credibility when you can share a story that's not just the same industry, but another branch of the prospect's own organization.

A CRM software company created a customer story featuring the success of one branch of a major nationwide mortgage company. The branch had become the number-one branch in the country largely due to productivity with the software. Using a success story on that branch, the software company got in the door with leaders at the national headquarters and are now in talks to take the software to more branches nationwide. "The success story has been extremely important in our sales efforts," the account rep noted.

Right Information, Right Time

To be effective in the sales process, customer stories have to deliver the right information at just the right time. Imagine managing customer stories for about one-hundred products and services, available in dozens of countries. That's the challenge for a large data-storage solutions company. The company's full-fledged customer-reference program, with thousands of customers, ensures that potential buyers have the opportunity to understand the experiences of current customers. Though they are just one of the reference team's responsibilities, customer stories are a significant piece of the program. The company currently has more than 550 customer stories–in written, video, and podcast formats–across its many products, services, customers, industries, and geographies. And the reference team continues to grow the databank of stories based on the field's needs.

When the company's customer reference program began in 2003, it used "customer profiles," two- to three-page customer stories that summarize the customer's relationship with company products and services. But the reference team heard grumbling from the company's field employees. "We were hearing discontent in the field that stories were not what they needed to help win business," says the director of the company's reference team. "The stories weren't that targeted to specific initiatives or products or proof points. It was just the story of their relationship with us."

Before creating more new stories, the company engaged Phelon Group (www.phelongroup.com) to take a more strategic approach. The firm helps organizations gather customer insight and key metrics to enhance customer retention, referability, and repurchase. Working together, they devised an online survey to poll the field about their use of and need for customer stories. Out of 6,000 sales reps, eleven percent across thirty-five countries completed the survey–an impressive response rate for busy reps focused on sales.

Here's what they learned:

- A small percentage uses the right tools at the right times during deals.
- Story access was the biggest challenge. Ease of access to stories was a bigger determinant of use than potential tool effectiveness.
- The field wanted more current and detailed stories.

In response, the company inventoried its existing stories and performed a strategic gap analysis to fill the voids. It also defined a "customer evidence model" to help reps understand when to leverage different types and lengths of customer stories based on time in the sales cycle and type of decision-maker:

Customer profile

Two- to three-page stories that highlight the challenge, solution, and benefits/metrics. Technical and business decision-makers consult these during the early awareness and interest phases as they explore solutions online.

Customer-solution showcase

Four to six pages that focus on the story of the solution, rather than the customer, using customer proof points to validate the solution. Available on the intranet for reps to use with business and technical audiences in the early part of the sales cycle.

Case study

Seven to ten pages focusing on either the implementation (event-focused) or the technical solution (product-focused). For use during evaluation and selection. On the company intranet.

Total cost of ownership (TCO) profile

The company works with a third-party ROI analysis firm to capture an unbiased view of the investment and returns for final decision-makers. Stories are ten to twenty pages and used during the evaluation, selection, and purchase phases. Accessible on the internal site.

With a broad mix of stories from which to choose, sales people have what they need, now easily accessible in a searchable online catalog that also includes video clips and podcasts of customer stories. Reps around the world can look for the stories they need by product, service, industry, type of story, language, and geography. As needed by regions, the company translates stories into different languages. But for new product rollouts, they create stories in all languages where they do business to ensure prospects understand new solutions.

Ultimately, the company hopes to minimize live one-on-one reference calls by talking to customers once and then creating a series of relevant stories that effectively give prospects a sense of what their experience might be as customers. "We're putting all this work into the upfront customer story development to ensure the field has a fully rounded portfolio of customer stories, and to negate the later need for a sales call to provide the proof points to customers. The stories show them other people are doing it successfully," says the director of the reference program.

Financing Proposals/Presentations

Making your case to banks, investors, or venture-capital firms is similar to the sales process. However, instead of selling them on specific products and services, you're selling them on the viability and potential profitability of your company. If you can demonstrate satisfactory and successful relationships with current customers, these parties have greater confidence in supporting your organization. For these contacts, leverage success stories to show short overviews of several customer relationships.

IMPACT-New Mexico Business Services (IMPACT-NM), the business services division of New Mexico Community Capital (www.nmccap.org), created a series of success stories featuring some of the small, rural New Mexico businesses it has assisted. The nonprofit provides hands-on business expertise from executives in the region, and thus represents an essential missing link in the development of New Mexico's economic infrastructure. Through "in the trenches" mentoring, IMPACT-NM delivers a full range of financial and development services to entrepreneurs, giving them critical customized assistance.

The organization provides business services that many New Mexico small businesses would not otherwise be able to afford. Client companies cover some of the cost of the services provided, while IMPACT-NM subsidizes the remainder. To do so, the organization needs to attract capital from investors interested in "double-bottom-line" benefits —the benefit of a return on the investment and the rewards of helping a company grow and create jobs in poor rural communities.

To approach investors and show its value to all stakeholders (employees, volunteers, board members, grant organizations), IMPACT-NM created several success stories on clients that grew their businesses with the assistance of the organization. For major investors in particular, the organization felt it needed well-written stories to show its value. "Now that we have compelling client stories explaining the power of our sustainable business services, a thorough business plan for IMPACT-New Mexico, and strategic and operating plans, we feel well-equipped to approach these people," says Leslie Elgood, Chief Operating Office and Nonprofit Director. "Because New Mexico Community Capital does not have a lengthy track record of service or the emotional appeal of many other non-profits (especially those that feed the hungry, serve children/families, do animal welfare, etc.), these stories are our way of creating both a strong business bond and an emotional bond. They *show* what we are accomplishing through client voices. They document the needs by using expert testimony— that of the service recipients."

IMPACT-NM leverages the stories in multiple ways: on its Web site; printed and paired with a one-page executive summary; a tool in fundraising meetings and conversations; for public relations and media inquiries; mailed with an introductory letter; and left behind in face-to-face meetings. In live conversations, the stories serve as launching points for specific discussions about client successes.

Teaching Sales Reps to Use Customer Stories

A lot of time and energy goes into producing strategically crafted customer stories. It's essential that sales reps understand how to use them to maximize sales opportunities. Many organizations include strategies for using customer stories as part of their sales training programs.

SAP AG (www.sap.com), the world's largest business software company, identified a need to train its sales representatives specifically on using its "reference assets," such as success stories and ROI case studies. "We knew that reference assets are one of the most powerful sales tools offered to the field, but learned that not all reps know how to effectively use the assets we offer," Erik Schulz, Vice President, Customer Value and Reference Services.

In 2006, SAP built and launched an online course as part of its SAP University, "How to Use Reference Assets in the Sales Cycle," which teaches reps how to use which assets for which purposes. The module is part of the optional curriculum for Sales & Marketing at SAP. Through surveys of the field, SAP has developed an understanding of when reps use the company's success stories and ROI case studies for the greatest impact. For example, success stories are applied most in the "Explaining" phase, while more extensive ROI case studies are used most in the "Proofing" phase. SAP shares those statistics with reps in its e-Learning class, as well as which assets are available to reps, ways to use them, different approaches for different customer segments, and how to nominate successful, happy customers for the reference program.

To make the content engaging, SAP chose an interview format whereby featured reps share their experiences and best practices from the field. It also includes mini case studies to help reps practice the newly learned skills. The training emphasizes careful selection of the right story for the optimum fit with the prospect. It's also available in a PowerPoint format for easy distribution and reference.

To date, the course has proven popular with reps. "The course is consistently one of the most frequently used eLearning assets our team provides," Schulz said.

Story-Selling for Independent Consultants

Customer examples in sales are just as essential for small businesses and independent consultants as they are for large companies. Anna Maravelas, President of TheraRising, Inc. (www.TheraRising.com) and author of *How to Reduce Workplace Conflict and Stress*, calls herself a "corporate peacemaker." Over the past twenty years, she has resolved countless work-place conflicts at organizations large and small, public and private.

Yet despite her success, she found that prospects had a hard time seeing the real value of her conflict-resolution consulting and seminars. To help them understand more clearly, she began capturing customer success stories to serve as important evidence that organizations pay a huge price for conflict in the work place.

"I began using written success stories out of the frustration I felt with people not recognizing how important the work was, and hesitating to spend the money when I knew in my heart of hearts that they were losing tens of thousands, hundreds of thousands or even millions of dollars in profit," Maravelas says.

Up to that point, Maravelas had leveraged her success stories verbally in conversations with potential clients. But several factors led her to put her stories in writing: a desire to document clients' cost savings; a need to show the details behind client results (how they got from point A to point B); a desire to focus on the prospect's current situation in discussions and leave customer examples behind for the prospect to read later; and concern about forgetting the nuances of various customer successes over time, if they weren't documented.

Due to the sensitive nature of conflict resolution, Maravelas leaves client names off her success stories, and writes them based on her project experience with customers, as opposed to interviewing client contacts again. She finds prospective clients, who face similar conflict issues, respect the need to keep client names confidential.

Of course, customer stories are just one part of her sales and marketing toolkit. "The story adds one piece to the puzzle that also includes the credibility of being interviewed in major publications," she says. "All of it says, 'I trust this woman. She seems competent.' It's a powerful combination."

She finds that written success stories also help her contacts sell her services to others in their organizations. They have documented cost-savings details from other companies to share with decision-makers. In addition to giving stories to prospects, she includes them on her Web site, and features many in her book. Those stories become interactive in her seminars. She tells the group about an actual work-place conflict, and then asks them to speculate what might be the hidden cause. Then, she provides the insight and outcome, which help the audience truly understand the concepts she's teaching. "I always try to highlight the stories that are touching, that appeal to our emotion and our desire to have lasting relationships," she says.

Anatomy of Customer-Story Use

So, how does a sales rep use a customer story in a typical sales process? Jim Conway, Account Manager, Energy for IHS Inc., is quite literally "in the field" every day. As he sells FieldDIRECT, an IHS service for capturing and storing oil and gas production data, he meets with foremen and pumpers in the fields of South Texas.

A thirty-year industry sales veteran, Conway believes strongly in using customer stories to help prospects understand exactly how they will benefit from using FieldDIRECT. "I use case studies in every presentation and in every conversation with prospects," Conway says. "They provide a lot of validity and credibility for our service."

After talking with a prospect by phone, Conway follows up that conversation with an email that includes product information, and three or four FieldDIRECT customer stories. For in-person meetings, he assembles a collection of materials on the FieldDIRECT service, such as a summary of the value proposition and benefits, along with printed versions of several customer stories. In presentations, he inserts brief customer examples in his PowerPoint slides. He pulls the most compelling proof points and testimonials from the customer stories to show how existing customers are successfully using the service in their workflow.

For one particular sales opportunity, Conway left behind his usual packet of materials that included the stories. "The decision-maker read every single line on the Web page and in all the materials I left," he says. "I feel like it was huge for those guys to be able to see how other companies are using the service." Conway landed the deal, a customer with the potential to bring as many as 1,000 wells into the IHS FieldDIRECT service.

To sell well with customer stories, Conway stresses he needs a portfolio of stories from which to choose. Whether he's meeting with a small, independent energy company or a major industry player, he can pull out a story that matches the prospect's situation. "When a prospect sees a similar client using the service successfully in their workflow, they can really see how they could gain from it," Conway says.

Whether your organization is large or small, you can leverage customer stories to help buyers get past the fear and uncertainty in purchase decisions. Customer stories and the content therein are valuable at every stage of the sales cycle; just choose the right type and amount of content to resonate with decision-makers as they move through the buying process.

Sub-Chapter Take-Aways

- Include customer stories as part of the sales training process to educate reps about the benefits and results that customers experience.

- Drop bite-sized pieces of customer proof points—on voice mail, email, or mail—when trying to get in the door with prospects.

- In the education/evaluation phase of the sales cycle, give prospects stories that answer their "how does it work" questions to help them narrow down to a short list.

- Help prospects validate the purchase with qualitative and quantitative results details that are important to the prospect.

- Determine what types of stories—in terms of length and type of content—are most influential at each part of the sales cycle.

- Regularly survey the field to understand how effective stories are for sales, and what gaps you need to fill.

- Leverage customer stories to up-sell to existing customers or to sell to other locations or divisions or an existing customer.

- Teach sales reps how and when to use stories, as well as where to access them.

Spinning Success Stories into Media Coverage

"Public relations is a form of classic storytelling, but for business...It doesn't matter if you're promoting a country, company, product, person or cause; if you tell the story with the same structure, elements, archetypes and path of all great stories, your message will be heard and acted on. And, in business, whoever tells the best story wins."

—Robbie Vorhaus, President and CEO,
Vorhaus & Company Inc.

As a business journalist, I was always on the hunt for engaging stories that no one had told yet. But those were the toughest story ideas to find. Usually, it meant calling around to various contacts and digging for in-the-trenches accounts of businesses facing and solving challenges. Rarely did anything like this come across my desk in a press release or a call from a company. Mostly, I heard about new hires, new products, or new facilities.

For some business audiences, the subjects contained in typical press releases are helpful—usually as lead sources for those looking to sell to businesses with new hires, new products, or new facilities. But many readers want insightful accounts of how other organizations are successfully navigating challenges. Pick up just about any business publication, or visit an online business site, and you'll find articles with success-story themes. A company solved a problem or overcame a challenge as a result of actions it took, or solutions implemented.

Chances are, you have a number of these types of stories among your customer base—accounts of customers doing business more productively, efficiently, or profitably as a result of a product or service you delivered. It's up to you to find those stories and bring them to the relevant media outlets.

"When PR agencies and businesses come to me with customer stories, I'm always interested," says Mila D'Antonio, Managing Editor of 1to1 Magazine (www.1to1media.com). "When you attach a customer story, it really helps bring to life a company's solution or initiative, or brings some cache. It's a challenge to get a good story if it doesn't have a good customer story in it."

Pitching to Editors

Providing a concrete story that's just perfect for a publication's audience goes a long way toward catching an editor's interest. For more than fifteen years, Bob Dirkes has helped companies get their best stories in front of editors. As an account manager at Tech Image, a Chicago-area technology PR firm, Dirkes and the team pitch stories to relevant media for clients every day–and prefer to do so with clients' customer success stories in hand. "If you parse out the story according to the interest and individual requirements of an editor, nothing goes further than a customer success story," Dirkes says. "Those stories are an important part of any business-to-business PR program. And a success story or case study format captures a customer's success story best because it's complete–problem, solution, and results. It's that complete storyline that's key with editors."

The firm actively relies on customer stories to help position its growing technology clients as market leaders. According to Dirkes, a flexible approach to stories gets the best results. As with any marketing communications, target and deliver the information according to the intended audience. For one editor, that might be offering bullet-point highlights that provide a quick overview. Another might like the story as a contributed article bylined by the most relevant customer contact at the featured organization. Or, a reporter may want the complete written story for background to shape her own interview and story.

Tech Image pays attention to editors' preferences and delivers client stories in the most appropriate format. In response, Dirkes finds the average story generates at least three media placements of some kind for clients. "Every success story or case study that we have ever pitched has found a home somewhere in some form," Dirkes says. "It's usually a three to one ratio, with one case generating at least three pieces of media coverage."

Customer-Story Mileage

But many customer stories generate far more than that. Tech Image broke down the coverage that resulted from using a single success story for a customer relationship-management (CRM) software client. Here's what happened when the firm turned it into a press release:

Press release picked up in eighteen different publications and Web sites, including DallasNews.com, Forbes.com, Morningstar.com, SFGate.com (*San Francisco Chronicle*), and Yahoo Finance. "These were wire pick-ups, which simply puts our client's name out there in a persistent positive way," Dirkes recalls. "We don't expect wire drops to generate higher quality stories. We just want continuing presence in what I call the 'Web & flow' of business news."

A writer for TMCnet wrote a column featuring the company based on the story told in the press release and case study.

BtoB magazine assigned a writer to cover it, leading to a nice piece in this widely read publication.

Finally, Tech Image used the written story to submit for and win a CRM Excellence Award for its client's technology.

According to Dirkes, it's the magic of the story that makes a difference with editors. Regardless of how or how many ways you plan to use a customer story, Dirkes stresses that the story must be captured in written form first. From there, it's always available and ready to be used in that format or easily repurposed. Plus, that written content, when launched into the online realm, is now readable by search engines. "If the story has never been captured, and it's just available anecdotally or in someone's PowerPoint presentation, it's not available to be used in all these different ways," Dirkes adds.

Small-Budget Media Relations

Small businesses, with equally small PR budgets, can also leverage customer stories to achieve media exposure. Jeff Fisher has always handled his own publicity for his Portland-based design firm, Jeff Fisher LogoMotives. Fisher designs corporate identities for companies of all types and sizes, and has racked up nearly 575 regional, national, and international graphic-design awards to date.

Fisher weaves in his customer stories in a number of ways. He sends out press releases promoting work with a specific client, and detailing the client project. In tying in with his Jeff Fisher LogoMotives business name, each release is complete with a "Toot! Toot!" at the top and a disclaimer at the end: "*If I don't "toot!" my own horn, no one else will.*"

Tech Image's 'Seven Ways to Slice a Customer Story'

Here are seven ways Tech Image flexibly uses success story and case study content according to various editors' needs and preferences:

Pitch the complete story—When a written story is a fit for a publication's audience, the firm might send it in its entirety to pique an editor's interest.

Quotes—Tech Image sometimes pulls out quotes to share with editors, rather than sending the full story.

Story highlights—Likewise, the firm at times extracts the "summary bullets" that often accompany customer stories. They perfectly encapsulate the results a featured customer has seen.

Prep clients for media interviews—"How do we prep our client subjects for interviews? Have them read their own success stories or case studies," Dirkes says. Before an executive meets with or speaks with an editor, Tech Image encourages him or her to read the company's customer stories so that anecdotes are top of mind and "conversations with editors are compelling."

Help reporters craft questions and stories—A written customer story provides valuable background to reporters as they prepare for interviews and craft their own stories.

Contributed articles—The firm helps repurpose clients' success stories and case studies into contributed articles written by someone at the featured customer organization.

Awards submissions—Countless publications and organizations offer industry awards programs, many of which are customer-story driven. Organizations should look for awards programs and categories that fit their stories. Some might highlight successful technology implementations, while others may emphasize results. Dirkes advises, "Every award has a formula. Study the program to discover the formula."

Fisher also integrates customer stories into articles he writes for magazines and Web sites, and in his own blogs. They also appear in his books, *The Savvy Designer's Guide to Success: Ideas and tactics for a killer career* and *Identity Crisis!: 50 Redesigns That Transformed Stale Identities into Successful Brands.* All of the above benefit Jeff Fisher LogoMotives' business and clients, often small businesses also wanting exposure.

In his thirty-year design career, Fisher has built quite a list of media relationships with industry media and contacts, as well as local and national publications. He focuses on fostering relationships, rather than just pursuing one-time PR. "In initiating a relationship with editors, I sometimes send them one of my marketing packets as an introduction," said Fisher, Engineer of Creative Identity for Jeff Fisher LogoMotives. "Close relationships with some editors/writers allows me to just pick up the phone and contact them immediately in some cases." He also takes advantage of press-release distribution sites such as PRLeap, and posts releases on Fast Pitch Networking, Facebook, MySpace, other social-networking sites, and design-industry Web portals. The biggest benefit of this is better search-engine rankings. At times, editors contact Fisher for additional information. Plus, potential clients more easily find his Web site, as do book authors looking for resources regarding graphic design.

From experience, Fisher has learned to have customer stories and approvals prepared for when media contacts call—on deadline—looking for stories. "In the past, this would result in going into panic mode, tracking down a client for approval to share information about a project and the success of that project, or trying to get signed permission from a client to use visuals from their business under tight editorial deadlines," he says.

Now, he speeds up the process and ensures he makes the most of PR opportunities with a succinct project agreement that covers PR:

"The designer retains personal rights to use the completed project and any preliminary designs for the purpose of design competitions, future publications on design, educational purposes and the marketing of the designer's business. Where applicable the client will be given any necessary credit for usage of the project elements."

Over the years, Fisher's persistent, diligent efforts have paid off with mentions in *USA Today*, *The Wall Street Journal* and *Fortune*, among others. "You never know who will be attracted to your press release information, and contact you, once the content is 'out there,'" he says.

Jeff Fisher's PR Pointers for Small Businesses

Learn to write a press release well, or develop a relationship with a professional who can put your thoughts into proper PR form.

Don't limit PR to local media. "Go for the big media resources in which you would like to see your business promoted. You never know what kind of story national media may be looking to publish."

ALWAYS carry your business cards with you to be ready for PR opportunities that pop up at any moment.

Keep in touch with media contacts on a regular basis, and develop relationships over time.

Don't be afraid to call up an editor, writer, or broadcast producer and ask if they would be willing to take the time for you to buy them a cup of coffee and pitch a story idea.

The Story Press Release

When approaching editors, some businesses share a full customer story as-is, tailor a customer-story press release to the specific publication, or send a summary of the story to determine the editor's interest. Many companies see PR results with a "story press release," a release that doesn't just talk about a product or service, but rather puts it in the context of a customer's setting. Instead of following a standard, formulaic press-release format, such releases tell a story about the customer's challenges, why the organization selected the vendor, and the results the customer has seen. For example, a release that announces you are working with a new customer or just completed a project with a specific customer can detail the customer's need for a solution and how your solution benefited the business. The same goes for product launches or newly offered services.

Media Targeting

As Tech Image and LogoMotives demonstrate, building relationships with targeted media and editors is the path to coverage. Research and reach out to the most important media outlets for your industry and offering, whether those are online, print, radio, or TV programs. Read, listen and watch their programming to see whether they cover the type of information you have to share, and the audience that you target. More than anything else, the audience must match.

Find out what types of stories your key media are looking for. D'Antonio of *1to1 Magazine* prefers customer stories that show the initial problems or challenges a business faced, and the solutions or recommendations applied to those problems. The best ones include specific return on investment or benefit details, she says. Once you know your best media contacts and preferences, create a personalized media list and maintain it continuously. Verify contacts regularly, or before each press release or pitch, as reporters and editors change.

For one-on-one story pitching, determine which media outlet will be the best fit. Call your contact to let them know you have a story that seems like a good match for the publication and its audience, then follow up with more information.

News-Release Distribution Services

You can also distribute press releases via wire services or other online services, which fill in the gaps with all those not on your personal media list. The conventional wisdom is that you can't really expect high-quality coverage in top media from simply sending out an announcement via the wire, but sometimes a press release will hit a media outlet with just the right information at just the right time, resulting in more than a small blurb. Also, sending out news releases via the wire blankets the Web with full press releases or shorter mentions of your company on news sites, improving search-engine optimization and directing more traffic back to your Web site.

The following are wire services and online press-release distribution sites. Some have fees while others are free, and have varying levels of media reach and targeting. Many of them even feature their own customer stories about their results on their Web sites.

PR Newswire, www.prnewswire.com

Business Wire, www.businesswire.com

PRWeb, www.prweb.com

Press Release, www.1888pressrelease.com

WebWire, www.webwire.com

eReleases, www.ereleases.com

PRLeap, www.prleap.com

Press Release, www.24-7pressrelease.com

Marketwire, www.marketwire.com

Send2Press.com, www.send2press.com

Click Press, www.clickpress.com/releases

Express Press Release, http://express-press-release.com

Free Press Release, www.free-press-release.com/submit/free-press-release.php

I-Newswire, www.i-newswire.com/submit_free.php

Media Post, www.mediapost.com

PR Free, www.prfree.com

The Web Wire, www.webwire.com

PR.com

SBwire.com

PRlog.com

i-Newswire.com

Today, you can set up alerts on sites such as Google.com (Google Alerts) to let you know when anything about your organization is published on the Web. Simply set up Google Alerts with keywords that are specific to your company and solutions. Likewise, media outlets and analysts in your industry may be using this feature to track news about organizations like you. That's another reason to ensure that your press releases include keywords.

First Right of Refusal

If the media aims to bring fresh information to its audiences, then many editors want stories that haven't run in other publications, or even on your Web site yet. That's why businesses and PR agencies often pitch customer stories to media contacts before they are published anywhere else. For your most coveted media contacts, present customer stories as "exclusives" and ensure they know that you are giving them the first right of refusal on a hot story idea.

Expect Media to Do it Their Way

You usually can't expect a publication, radio, or TV program to run your customer story exactly as you deliver it. If you want it precisely in your words and format, then it's best to pay for an advertorial. When reporters cover your story, they do so to fit their own objectives, audiences, and editorial formats, rather than to sell your products or services. Hence, the focus will usually be on a particular business topic or your customer, with your name and solutions as mentions in the story. Your customer and solutions may even be a one-sentence or one-paragraph mention in a broader story on a related topic—and may also include competitive solutions. But that's still very valuable publicity.

Anticipate Media Interviews

Editors and reporters also usually take control of information-gathering for their own stories, instead of trusting what's in a story you provided them. In most cases, a success story or case study serves as a means of "pitching" your story idea to an editor, who will then assign a reporter to cover it. Most publications have teams of staff or freelance writers who will take your story as background information, or as the concept of the story, and write their own versions. They do this for a number of reasons. By interviewing subjects and crafting their own stories, they ensure that the story they put out is fresh and hasn't run anywhere else, that it has the angles and information that will interest the audience, and that the sources and data are credible. It gives them the chance to verify the accuracy of information. They can't risk their reputations by printing inaccurate information.

A media outlet could cover your organization or customer story without additional interviews, but many writers and editors will conduct their own additional interviews to fit their angles and audiences, and to confirm the facts are correct.

When you create press releases from a customer story, check with the relevant contacts at client organizations to ensure they are comfortable talking with reporters. If you know ahead of time, you can simply give reporters contact information or arrange a call, instead of having to take the time to call your contacts and make sure they are willing to talk after a reporter asks. If reporters are on deadline—and they always are—they don't have time to wait.

Contributed Articles

With the Web, more media outlets than ever are looking for fresh content: the online sites of traditional media, news portals, industry sites, blogs, e-newsletters, and more. No longer limited to just the amount of space in a magazine, newspaper, or a thirty-minute radio show, they need content continuously. Quite a few take contributed articles, which are authored and submitted by outside parties not staffed or hired by the media outlet.

You often see contributed articles in business and trade publications. Too often, they rehash information readers have heard before, just said in a different way. Here, a powerful customer story can really make an article stand out and provide the concrete examples that readers need. Typically, a contributed article from your organization would be "by-lined" (as in "By Mary Smith") by someone within your company. However, when turning a customer story into an article, it's much more credible and powerful with most editors for your main customer contact to be the author. If you already have that customer story written, it's a simple process to repurpose it as an article written by your customer contact.

Editorial Guidelines

First, find out if key publications covering your subject accept contributed articles. Study the publication's content and read the blurbs at the end of articles that describe the authors. Those written by outside individuals usually include the author's brief bio, title, and organization at the end. Next look for editorial guidelines that define how the publication approaches contributed articles. Those guidelines usually provide details on how to get prior approval for your article, along with specifics regarding deadlines, word counts, and what type of content isn't allowed. Typically, publications are very strict about overtly pushing products, services, or companies.

Also look for editorial calendars. Many publications have schedules of the topics they plan to cover throughout the year with each issue. Much of the content and advertising will tie into each theme, giving contributors an opportunity to find the most relevant topical issues for which to submit articles. If an editor likes your story idea, find out the exact deadline and don't miss it!

The Publication's Style

A customer story usually needs some reworking to transition into an article format. The style, length, and format should match that of the intended publication and audience, rather than your own format. Instead of your product or service being the star of the show, your customer's business challenges and results move into focus. If you don't already use short paragraphs in your customer story, shorten paragraphs to match journalism style. Finally, make sure the article speaks specifically to the publication's readers.

Journalism Style

When you submit a press release or article to an editor, it helps to follow standard journalism style—and may even impress an editor. While this doesn't make or break your chances of securing media coverage, it might help with those publications interested in running your story as-is. Many publications will write their own stories, but sometimes they simply run entire press releases or parts of press releases. If the information already follows clean journalism style, it's that much easier to pop it into their publications quickly.

The *Associated Press Stylebook,* sometimes called "the journalist's bible," has become the standard for journalism style for most publications. You should be able to find it easily on the shelves of your local bookstore or online. Journalism-style rules dictate exactly how your words, numbers, titles, and proper names should read in print. For example, numbers from one to nine are spelled out, while those over ten are written as numerals. Titles are lowercase when separated from the person's name in a sentence by a comma, as in Mary Smith, vice president of marketing.

Style guides are primarily used to ensure that all content in a publication is consistent. Whether you use AP Style or not *does not usually* determine an editor's decision to pursue your story. However, if your document is full of inconsistencies or poor style, it can turn an editor off. As a business journalist, I often tossed really sloppy press releases I received because they indicated companies didn't care or didn't take the time to ensure that the information they sent out was presented cleanly and professionally.

Many companies have created their own style guides to dictate how their product names and phrases should look, and trade marking. For example, they might prefer "website" over the AP Style treatment, "Web site." Using your own style, as long as its clean and professional, shouldn't affect your coverage. It just might mean that publications wanting to run your press release verbatim need to edit it to fit their own style first.

Reprints

Online and traditional media can have strict rules regarding reprinting articles, linking to them from your Web site or e-newsletters, and using their logos. Find out the rules and make sure you follow them to keep in their good graces. Reprints may cost you, so decide how you plan to use those articles and weigh the benefits versus the cost.

Publications that cover your industry or your customer's industry want engaging stories about your customers. The formula is crafting a solid story, presenting it to the right media, and pitching it to them in their preferred manner.

Sub-Chapter Take-Aways

- Editors are looking for stories that show how an organization solved a problem or overcame a challenge as a result of actions it took, or solutions implemented.

- Give editors a complete story: problem, solution, and results.

- Get to know publications' preferences and provide customer-story details in the way each prefers—bulleted highlights, press release, or contributed article.

- Foster relationships with editors and reporters, rather than just pursuing one-time PR.

- If you have a small PR budget, consider using press-release distribution sites such as PRWeb.com, PRLeap.com, or social networking sites like Facebook and MySpace.

- Wire services and other press-release distribution services may not land the best coverage, but they help blanket the Web with mentions of your organization.

- Many companies see PR results with a "story press release," a release that doesn't just talk about a product or service, but rather puts it in the context of a customer's setting.

- Track your online coverage by setting up alerts for keywords and phrases with Google Alerts.

- Offer a story to your favorite publication(s) first. Some even want stories before they go on your Web site.

- Anticipate that publications may want to conduct their own interviews of your customers.

- Turn a customer story into a contributed article by-lined by your customer contact.

Telling Tales to Further Causes

"Even if you have reams of evidence on your side, remember: numbers numb, jargon jars, and nobody ever marched on Washington because of a pie chart. If you want to connect with your audience, tell them a story."

—Andy Goodman, author, *Storytelling as Best Practice*

Visit the Web site of most charities or public-interest groups and you'll likely find numbers, lots of numbers. Nonprofits use facts and data to illustrate the extent of the problems they're trying to solve. Ninety million children go hungry every day... someone will develop Alzheimer's every thirty-three seconds...While the numbers do support the need for action, they don't get audiences emotionally engaged and ready to take action.

The individual story or experience "always trumps the facts," says Andy Goodman, author of *Storytelling as Best Practice* (www.agood manonline.com). Goodman helps public-interest groups, foundations, and businesses reach more people more effectively—with storytelling as the primary means of achieving those goals.

While storytelling for causes resembles that of for-profit organizations in many ways, some distinctions exist. There's usually more emotion involved in supporting a cause than in buying software or consulting services. This sub-chapter sheds light on how nonprofit or public-interest communication varies and how to communicate your cause through stories.

A Face on the Problem

A lifelong humanitarian, Mother Teresa may have also been a natural at marketing. "If I look at the mass, I will never act. If I look at the one, I will," she is quoted as saying. This single statement effectively sums up what it means to communicate about causes. People aren't moved by sweeping statistics about thousands of affected individuals or acres of forest in danger. They're motivated by one man trying to survive cancer or a mama kit fox keeping herself and her litter safe as the forest disappears.

The book *Made to Stick* provides an example that underlies the importance of putting a face on the problem. The book highlights a Carnegie Mellon University study designed to understand what makes people act. Researchers asked people to complete a survey about technology (the survey's subject matter was irrelevant). At the end, they gave each participant five one-dollar bills, along with an envelope with a charity request to donate to Save the Children. Some included a letter that highlighted the problems facing children as a whole in Africa. Another included information about one affected girl. On average, those receiving the first letter gave $1.14 to the cause, while the ones receiving the second letter contributed $2.38. Effectively, the second letter put a human face on the cause—what amounted to the highlights of a girl's story—helping readers establish an emotional connection to the issue.

Person-to-Person Connections

Save the Children has been successful by communicating about individual children and enabling people to assist children on that one-on-one basis. Other organizations have adopted similar formats. Today, Kiva (www.kiva.org) combines this powerful concept with the reach of the Internet to enable the developed world to assist entrepreneurs in the developing world.

Started in 2005 by Matt and Jessica Flannery, Kiva empowers businesses and individuals to loan money directly to entrepreneurs in need around the world. Lenders can peruse a database of business owners across dozens of countries and industries, and read stories and view snapshots of each. The stories shed light on each entrepreneur's business, family life, challenges, and how they plan to use the loan. That element of story is central to the entire Kiva concept, such that, it's nearly impossible to imagine the nonprofit working without stories.

Each profile gives the entrepreneur's requested amount, ranging anywhere from twenty-five dollars to $1,200 each, with an average of $500-600. Lenders choose one or more entrepreneurs to support and then loan online. One or two dozen individual lenders typically contribute to reach the total requested, giving as little as twenty-five dollars each. Throughout the course of the loan (usually six to twelve months), lenders can receive email journal updates (more stories) from the businesses they've sponsored. As entrepreneurs repay loans, lenders get their loan money back or can loan again to another entrepreneur. To date, the concept has been remarkably effective for Kiva. The organization receives well over one million dollars in loans every month.

Organizations such as Save the Children and Kiva have been remarkably successful by letting individuals support specific individuals—and by telling the stories of those individuals in need.

"There's this really strong feeling of your contribution actually having an impact because you can see the effect of it immediately," said Fiona Ramsey, PR Manager at Kiva. "There's the immediacy of seeing your loan bump up the total online, and then the immediacy of receiving an email that says, 'Mary in Kenya just made a ten-dollar repayment on her loan.' We're connecting in the form of stories."

One lender, Diane, writes on the site: "I still come back to the faces of those whose loans I've helped fund...I read the human stories at Kiva.org and realize just how far a small amount of money can stretch for someone who is striving to work to better themselves and their families and their communities...and their world."

I personally became a Kiva lender when moved by the stories of two entrepreneurs, one in Tajikistan and another in Sierra Leone. I loaned a small amount to a woman business owner in Tajikistan, along with twenty-seven other people, all of us helping her reach her goal of $1100 to buy more inventory for her clothing business. I also chose a man in Sierra Leone with a general store who began the business when he could not continue his education. He too needed a loan to invest in more inventory to grow. Seven other people helped him reach his goal of $200. As they repay their loans and accomplish their goals, I receive email updates, allowing me to feel connected to these hard-working entrepreneurs in another culture.

In addition to entrepreneur stories, there's an element of story among lenders. When I log into the site, I can see all the other lenders and click for more information about them, including their photos, locations, occupations, why they lend, and any other entrepreneurs they support.

In addition to the connection I feel with entrepreneurs, I share solidarity with these many lenders who joined me in assisting these specific individuals—forging community in the developed world as well.

Kiva's use of entrepreneur and lender stories and photos gives lenders an important connection with entrepreneurs in the developing world and each other, making the experience more personal, and hence rewarding, for lenders.

Humanizing Heroes

Goodman asserts that every organization should find a way to communicate in human terms such as this. "People relate to people, so stories about your work—*any* line of work, really—must provide human protagonists to draw the audience in and lead them through the narrative," Goodman wrote in his monthly *free-range thinking*™ newsletter. "Even if your organization (a) is devoted to saving flora and/or fauna, (b) toils in the dense thicket of policy change, or (c) helps other organizations work more effectively, *human beings are still driving the action.*"

Alternatively, he says, your protagonists should have human qualities, so that readers have human characteristics to associate with. Think Smokey the Bear (who's real name was actually "Smokey Bear"), the spokes-bear for one of the longest-running public-service campaigns in U.S. history. Smokey seemed just as human as any of us, and hence helped reduce the number of forest fires significantly in North America.

In the past few years, Environmental Defense Fund (www.edf.org) has achieved a number of environmental successes by leveraging stories in nearly every communication with members, donors, and policymakers. The national nonprofit, with more than 500,000 members, brings together science, economics, law, and innovative private-sector partnerships to create solutions to the most serious environmental problems.

While the organization's cause is not directly about people—compared to organizations such as Save the Children or Kiva—Environmental Defense Fund stresses the human impact of all its issues. To explain the dangers of pollution and climate change, the organization's Web site tells the stories of a girl who can no longer play soccer because of Los Angeles air quality; of a skier and ski-industry businesses affected by warmer weather; and of families uprooted by hurricanes.

Likewise, you'll find stories and photos of scientists, businesspeople, policymakers, and regular citizens featured in the nonprofit's annual report, newsletters, direct-mail appeals, videos, press releases, presentations, and in one-on-one discussions with potential donors or legislators.

"Very few audiences are not moved by stories. They get people to pay attention to your message," says Peter Klebnikov, Editor in Chief at Environmental Defense Fund. "We often use humans to illustrate and inject a dynamic element and drama into what is a rather dry, scientific story and put problems in terms audiences can understand."

Universal Tales of Survival

Klebnikov says stories help raise money, attract allies, and sway decision makers. For one campaign, a compelling story did all three. In 1967, the San Joaquin kit fox was one of the first animals to be listed as an endangered species. However, the little, large-eared fox of Northern California remains in danger due to habitat loss caused by agricultural and industrial development, urbanization, and fragmentation of its habitat by roads. The kit foxes are finding fewer places to hide from predators such as coyotes and red foxes.

In response, Environmental Defense Fund launched a story-based campaign, telling the tale of this small fox trying to make it. "It was a universally appealing story of a small animal eeking out a survival against larger predators," Klebnikov said. The campaign included a direct-mail appeal that ended up being the most successful fundraising tool of that year. Ultimately, that resulted in a Safe Harbor agreement to benefit the endangered San Joaquin kit fox, whereby landowners agreed to take actions to protect the fox. That meant installing artificial kit fox dens to serve as refuges as foxes move across the agricultural lands—to literally outfox predators.

Another Environmental Defense Fund victory resulted from telling the story of a fisherman and his crew who spent nine hours in a life raft at sea as a result of misguided fishing regulations. In what's called a "derby," all fishermen were compelled to go out and catch as many red snapper as possible regardless of how bad the weather is, during a season that often lasted just a few days. The practice put fishermen in danger, depleted fish populations, and forced fishermen to waste a lot of other varieties of fish. After his fishing boat capsized in stormy weather in the Gulf of Mexico, forcing captain and crew to endure the storm in a lifeboat, the captain was convinced that new fishing policies were the answer. If not forced to earn a living in a short timeframe, he would not have gone out to sea in the storm. By sharing his story (also a tale of survival against forces of nature) with Environmental Defense Fund, which in turn told that story to federal policymakers, the nonprofit was influential in changing fishing policies to protect fishermen and fish.

The Nuances of Cause Storytelling

These types of emotional, human tie-ins are critical to garnering support for causes, yet many organizations don't promote their causes with stories, or don't do it enough, says Katya Andresen, author of *Robin Hood Marketing* and VP Marketing, Network for Good (www.networkforgood.org). "If you look at the Web sites of fifty small nonprofits, you would be hard-pressed to find written stories or pictures that tell a story," she says. "You should never be communicating without stories—pictures, examples or full-blown stories."

Andresen's book highlights the ways in which nonprofits can leverage marketing best practices from the corporate world. Organizations encounter some of the same challenges as companies in capturing their stories, but also some that are unique to nonprofits.

In the Weeds

Nonprofits can lose sight of what is extraordinary in their work, because they experience it everyday, Andresen says. "They're so far down in the weeds that they take stories for granted and don't recognize them as interesting anymore." She also points out that many hesitate to capture their stories because they worry they are "too simplified or individualized to capture the grand scheme of what they're trying to accomplish as an organization."

Limited Resources

In resource-challenged charitable organizations, there's rarely enough time or money to seek out the best success stories, and write and design them professionally. But in many cases, the raw voice of those you assist is the most effective presentation, rather than a polished marketing document.

Find creative ways of collecting those first-hand stories directly from beneficiaries. For example, encourage people to submit their own stories on your Web site. Organizations such as the Girl Scouts and Families USA have links where site visitors can tell their own stories. The former collects positive Girl Scout alumnae memories while the latter looks for health-care hardship stories to illustrate everyday struggles. As members, beneficiaries, or the public submit their stories, make sure you get clearance from them to use their stories publicly on your Web site, or include an option for them to go unnamed.

Before those are published on your site, have someone review them to ensure they reflect your mission, and correct any grammar, spelling, or punctuation errors. Establish a simple format in which to display every story, keeping it low maintenance for staff. This way, you effectively put storytelling in the hands of the people.

Other Sources for Story Ideas

Consider ways to encourage volunteers, board members, and sponsors to bring stories forward. Because they are not entrenched in the daily operations of the organization, they may be better suited to recognize powerful stories and pass those along. Along those lines, gather stories from these folks via "Share Your Story" links on your site as well. Encourage them to submit information that characterizes why they support your organization.

For more polished stories, or stories written in third person, engage professional writers and designers. To keep costs down, consider hiring a local journalism, PR, or design student looking for real-world experience. If you publish those stories in your newsletter, online, and other printed materials, the student has valuable content for his or her portfolio. Or, find someone among your volunteer or supporter base with storytelling experience willing to capture those stories as they surface. Just ensure anyone you engage to tell your stories understands your mission and the key points that you want to emphasize.

Doom and Gloom Themes

Andresen also cautions against being too negative in trying to illustrate problems. "There are 1.5 million nonprofits in the U.S.," she says. "Everyone needs money. Need is not enough. You can go gloom and doom, but so can 1.5 million other nonprofits. Donors need a dose of inspiration."

Too much negativity, making the problem seem overwhelming, gives audiences a helpless feeling. Andresen suggests touching on problems and negative consequences, but quickly moving on to how those problems have been solved. "Tell them what's wrong and then show them how they can set things right," she says.

Show Setbacks

Showing pitfalls and setbacks that people in your stories encountered makes them even more human for readers. Before reaching solutions, those in your stories may have tried many things. Goodman recommends including those twists and turns, rather than omitting them. Maybe the protagonists set out to solve a problem and encountered challenges or made mistakes along the way. Those types of hurdles, and what people learn as a result, create interest for readers. "It's the mistakes and opposition where it gets interesting," Goodman says. "People are afraid to let others know they have made mistakes, but it makes it real."

Use Aliases as Needed

Due to the nature of many causes, those who have been served by nonprofits may not want to share their stories publicly. Always respect those preferences and find ways to bring the information forward without naming those helped by your organization. The typical way is by changing the names of those featured or interviewed in your communications, with an asterisk note at the bottom indicating the person's name has been changed. Audiences seem to understand the reasons for keeping names anonymous in nonprofit communications, and it doesn't seem to hurt credibility to do so.

However, when it makes sense and when beneficiaries give their permission, bringing those individuals forward can make a powerful statement—and even be empowering for the person sharing her story. At a cancer fundraiser, it's moving to hear from people who have survived the disease. Or to read a letter published in a newsletter from a young woman who was able to go to college due to a scholarship from an organization. A number of people have become the "heroes" and spokespeople for Environmental Defense Fund campaigns, including the fisherman who felt strongly about changing fishing regulations and a former schoolteacher campaigning for cleaner air. In fact, the organization brings them to Washington to meet directly with senators and representatives.

Unexpected Story Perspectives

In addition to the direct beneficiaries of their services, nonprofits and public-interest groups have multiple audiences: donors, members, volunteers, and employees. Anecdotes about end beneficiaries only show part of the picture. It's also important to showcase volunteer, donor, and member stories to help potential volunteers, donors, and members understand the experience and rewards.

A 'Wish' Story

The Make-A-Wish Foundation (www.wish.org) has a long history of using stories about the children it helps, and has branched out to showcase stories on its donors, sponsors, volunteers, and "wish-granting stars." The organization, which grants wishes for children with life-threatening medical conditions, learned early on the power of the story—that of the first "wish kid."

In 1980, a seven-year-old boy from Phoenix, Arizona, named Chris Greicius realized his lifelong wish to become a police officer. Arizona Department of Public Safety officers joined to plan a day for the boy being treated for leukemia. It included a helicopter tour of the city, a visit to department headquarters, a swearing in as the first honorary DPS patrolman in state history, a custom-tailored DPS uniform, and a proficiency test on a battery-operated motorcycle.

Soon after that, Chris passed away. To honor his memory, his mother, Linda Bergendahl-Pauling, teamed with a DPS officer and an undercover security officer to form the Chris Greicius Make-A-Wish Memorial. By 1982, the group had granted eight wishes to children in the Phoenix area when Chris's story and those of the other children caught the attention of *NBC Magazine*, a national news program. Millions of people learned about Chris and how granting a single wish brings joy to children and their families. Just a year after the NBC story aired, the Make-A-Wish Foundation of America was officially incorporated, six official Make-A-Wish chapters were operating around the country, and twenty-two more were established the following year.

Today, Make-A-Wish grants a child's wish about every forty minutes. Only limited by a child's imagination, wishes range from meeting celebrities to taking a trip to having a dream experience like being a chef or a princess for a day. Because every wish has a compelling story behind it, it simply made sense to leverage the foundation's wish kid stories to reinforce its message, according to Mike Pressendo, Director of Brand Communications. "We're in an enviable position because everything we do has a great story associated with it," he says.

It's the extensive use of its stories that sets Make-A-Wish apart. On a visit to the foundation's Web site, the first thing you see is a large photo from a recent wish-granting. When you click on the photo, you are taken to the full story about the featured child's wish experience. From there, you can read one story after another. In fact, you could spend all day on the site reading different stories. About seventy-five percent of the stories on the site cover wish kids with the rest focusing on sponsors, volunteers, wish-granters, and donors. From the home page, you can also choose to read wish stories by type, from recent wishes to adventure themes to career-oriented wishes.

Ways Make-A-Wish Foundation Uses Child, Donor or Wish-Granter Stories

Web site home page and throughout

Electronic and print newsletters

Direct mail

Annual report

Training for new employees and volunteers

Press releases

Print, radio, and TV advertising

Public-service announcements

Live events

Phone "hold" message

Beyond the Web site, the foundation tells those stories in electronic and print newsletters, in the annual report, in training new employees and volunteers through an online learning system, and in public relations. Make-A-Wish tracks 400-600 print stories every month, not counting TV and radio coverage.

With limited on-staff writing and photography resources, the various chapters capture and send their stories to the national office. To assist those offices, the foundation created a business-card-sized cheat sheet with story-writing tips on one side and photography tips on the other. By the nature of the Make-A-Wish mission, everyone knows these children face challenges. Instead of focusing on the illness, the organization reinforces its brand message by highlighting the joy that the child and family experienced, or the joy of supporting the foundation.

Wish-granter campaign

In 2006, Make-A-Wish set out to increase its wish-granting resources significantly by adding volunteers, donations, frequent-flyer miles, and any other valuable resources to make wishes happen. In response, Make-A-Wish created a new campaign, Destination Joy℠ presented by LAY'S®, to inspire and empower Americans to share their much-needed time, talents, and resources. Instead of focusing on wish kids, the campaign showcases the organization's volunteer wish-granters to communicate the benefits that volunteers receive in the process of helping kids, and just how easy it is to help out. "Destination Joy tells the story through the eyes of the volunteers and those who get on board, and the joy it brings them as well," says Jennifer Maher, VP of Marketing and Corporate Alliances.

Make-A-Wish polled chapters to find the most moving stories of people granting wishes. In return, it uncovered a number of inspiring individuals and organizations to feature. The foundation executes the campaign through just about every type of media available, including online, TV, radio, and print public-service announcements. Most feature the photo, if not also the story, of a wish-granter: the high school teacher who played arch villain for a day to bring to life a six-year-old boy's wish to be a super hero; the baker who let a young boy and his friends join him in the kitchen; and a fashion photographer who helped a teenage girl be a supermodel for a day. The same message repeats on every story: "We all have the power to help children with life-threatening conditions. We all have the power to grant a wish."

When the marketing team started the campaign, they set out to increase the base of wish-granters by 20,000 in five years. After just two months, they had generated over 8,000 new supporters. The real stories, told clearly and consistently, gave power to the Make-A-Wish message. "When people read the stories, they think, 'I want to be a part of that.' For the first year, the results are astronomical," Maher said.

Ways to Use Stories

Story use for nonprofits and other public-interest groups closely resembles that of for-profit organizations. Here are some of the ways nonprofits and public-interest groups can leverage their customer-story content:

Employee/Volunteer Orientation

Marketing and development teams are usually accustomed to leveraging stories in their communications. Yet, numerous other staff and supporters could be spreading your message with success stories, including donors, sponsors, and volunteers. If one of your volunteers or donors speaks to a friend about your cause, he should be able to talk effectively about the organization's mission and the value that brings to beneficiaries. Those outside supporters serve as walking, talking bearers of the message in the public, so they need powerful stories in their back-pockets.

First, use your stories to train all employees, board members, major sponsors, and volunteers. As does oral tradition, hearing those stories gives them powerful anecdotes they can remember more easily and share with others. The president of Environmental Defense Fund holds a "fireside chat" once a year with all new employees. They are introduced to the organization's most important stories, which builds team spirit and "makes them proud to work there," Klebnikov says.

After the initial orientation, continue to share new stories in staff meetings, board meetings, and other meetings with volunteers, as well as with major sponsors and donors. They need to continue hearing those anecdotes to stay energized and inspired about your mission.

Web Site

While your Web site may not be the first impression people have of your organization, it's where they go for most of the information. Other mailings or communications efforts pique their interest, but the Web site provides the next level of detail. Make stories visible and accessible *right on the home page*, either in the form of a photo that reflects a story, a video, or the start of a written story that links to more detail. Organize stories by type, such as those you serve, donors, members, volunteers, etc., or by other relevant factors such as type of service you provide, constituents helped, geography, or ages.

Try to include photos that tell a story, rather than show your building or a board meeting. Decide what's more effective for your cause: snapshots taken by amateurs in the field or photos captured by professional photographers. Kiva and Make-A-Wish Foundation typically choose to go with more casual photos partly for greater authenticity and partly because of the difficulty of getting professional shots of those they assist. Environmental Defense Fund typically uses more professional photos to lend credibility to communications going to audiences such as policy-makers, corporations, and scientists. "We spend a lot of money on photography," says Klebnikov. "Today's culture is visual."

Fundraising Appeals

Too many fundraising appeals, typically delivered by email or regular mail, paint grim pictures of the problem at hand. Strike a balance between showing there's a problem—not *too* graphically—and indicating how your organization was part of the solution. Audiences need to see that happy ending in order to understand how the organization can help and that there are success stories result. You can include numbers, but remember data is hollow without stories to put faces behind the numbers.

Find creative ways of telling stories in fundraising appeals. Perhaps start out with the success part of the story and then touch on how far the person, business, animal, forest, or whatever you're benefiting has come. Tell your stories in third person, interview style, or in first person written by the person you helped or someone involved. Try different formats to determine the most effective for your audience.

Grant Proposals

In the competitive bid for grants, powerful stories help your proposals stand out. There's a place for facts and figures, but bring those numbers to life with stories that show the problem and highlight your ability to make a difference.

"A lot of foundations are very understaffed. They receive enormous amounts of material, often unsolicited. They may receive fifty to sixty proposals or more in the mail on a given day," says Ed Mohylowski, Director of Institutional Giving at Environmental Defense Fund. "There's a very good chance, that given the volume of proposals received, foundation staff will not read them, or if they do, they're going to do so very selectively—skimming those that meet the guidelines for highlights on who you are and what you need. If the proposal is well written and compelling, they may read it, and anecdotes do help very much, especially if accompanied with illustrations to catch people's eyes."

Mohylowski, with nearly fifteen years of fundraising experience, has always enhanced proposals with stories. "Storytelling is integral to the process of raising money," he says. "We have to demonstrate a need for whatever grant we are seeking and often a story that illustrates a success or underscores the depth of a problem will enhance the quality of the proposal and makes it much more compelling."

"Problem" stories paint a picture of need, while "success" stories show your ability to achieve positive outcomes. With entities that have not funded your organization previously, it gives them a sense of your capabilities. Existing grantors will see the outcomes attributable to the funds they gave.

Use Stories Wisely in Proposals

Environmental Defense makes stories personal, pulling in anecdotes of real people to enliven proposals. However, Mohylowski recommends choosing examples selectively, so as not to overwhelm or lose readers. Sometimes you may not have a choice in the length of your stories. Since many grant applications limit the amount of information you can provide, you may need to condense stories into two or three sentences or touch on them in the cover letter.

Newsletters/Magazines

Every newsletter that goes out to employees, members, volunteers, sponsors, donors, and any other constituents should include a story, if not multiple stories. We all receive way too much email and postal mail, so newsletters must stand out by including more than news blurbs or chapter updates. Again, include photos to draw readers into the story. If it's an email newsletter, perhaps include a short blurb and then a link that takes readers back to the longer story on your Web site.

I remember one issue in particular of The Humane Society of the United States's (www.hsus.org) quarterly magazine, *All Animals*. When Hurricane Katrina hit the Gulf Coast, the Humane Society reacted quickly to save thousands of animals. The following year, an issue of their magazine featured several heartwarming stories of rescues and reunions between pets and their owners. For people displaced by the storm, reunion with their pets was a huge step toward recovery. For me, already a member, the stories reinvigorated my dedication to the organization.

Annual Reports

Environmental Defense Fund communicates that it brings together Ph.D. scientists, economists, and business experts to work together to solve environmental problems. Its annual report not only showcases successes, but shows how these broad partnerships between diverse parties brought about results.

The organization's full-color annual report has engaging photos (some of them large-format) of the people who have been active in Environmental Defense Fund initiatives. It also includes some of each year's results in feature-story format, as well as updates on ongoing issues. Finally, the financial stats come at the end. By leading with people and stories, the annual report succeeds in connecting with people on an emotional level before presenting the requisite financial details.

Advertising/Public-Service Announcements

Public-service announcements (PSA) for print, radio, or television are perfect opportunities to tell a story quickly. Make-A-Wish Foundation created one-page, color print advertisements featuring wish-granters and short stories about them, as well as thirty- and sixty-second radio and TV PSAs that briefly capture stories about wish-granters.

Speeches and Meetings

Tell a story in a room full of people or in an important donor meeting, and chances are, you will keep them engaged, connect with them on an emotional level, and get your message across. Encourage a culture of storytelling not only in marketing communications, but in all face-to-face and even phone opportunities.

Understand your audience and try to choose stories that mean something to them, or that will be universally appealing. If you "break the ice" with a powerful account of how your organization made a difference, then the door is open for your appeal or request.

Your Physical Environment

Andresen points out another area where many nonprofits fail to communicate—their offices. Your lobby and offices should have pictures and other communications that easily and quickly communicate who you are and what you accomplish.

Your Hold Message

Take advantage of another inexpensive way to reach your audience—your phone hold message. If you call the Make-a-Wish Foundation headquarters, you may hear the voices of wish kids within seconds. The organization's hold messages are real wish kids talking about their wish experiences and how that made them feel. It's a powerful reminder of the joy Make-A-Wish Foundation brings.

Public Relations

The media lives for compelling stories. After all, that's what their audiences want. That's why your outbound communications efforts, either formatted in press releases, emailed, or verbally communicated to media contacts, will make a bigger impression if you tell a story, rather than just giving facts. Find ways to weave relevant, real anecdotes into your press releases. Don't be afraid to start your press release with a powerful anecdote to get readers engaged. Having worked on both sides of the fence—as a journalist and media-relations contact for a nonprofit educational organization—I've seen the impact of beginning a press release with a related anecdote and then tying in your announcement or message.

Then there are more passive, yet still very effective, ways of generating media coverage with stories. The Make-A-Wish Foundation doesn't even pitch most of its wish kid and other success stories. The media finds them on the national Web site or on local branch sites.

This is where a searchable story bank is particularly valuable. You can handle your story bank a couple of ways. Either allow constituents to submit their own stories online, which you verify for authenticity, grammar, and punctuation, and make active and searchable to the public. Or, you can create stories that you post online and make searchable to the public.

Again, when you receive or collect stories, make sure you get clearance from those featured to use their stories publicly, and let them know that could include being contacted by the media. This effectively allows for media self-service. When a reporter is looking for a story about a particular topic in your area, he can easily find it in your data bank, anytime of the day or night. Just make sure you review your story bank frequently and remove any information that no longer supports your mission or is outdated.

As evidenced by the successes of these nonprofits and causes, stories add a compelling component to your communications efforts, putting an essential face on the numbers and inspiring action.

Sub-Chapter Take-Aways

- Put a face on the problems your organization addresses, and its successes.

- Humanize heroes, even if they're animals or inanimate objects.

- Find creative ways of collecting first-hand stories directly from beneficiaries, such as Share Your Story links on your Web site.

- Encourage volunteers, board members, and sponsors to bring stories forward. Those not entrenched in the daily operations of the organization may be better suited to recognize powerful stories when they hear them.

- Keep themes positive, rather than doom and gloom.

- Tell the stories of others involved in your organization, such as donors, volunteers, and other supporters, beyond just those who benefit from your services.

- Tell a story in all your communications media.

10

Creating Connections with Stories

"The story—from Rumplestiltskin to War and Peace—is one of the basic tools invented by the human mind, for the purpose of gaining understanding. There have been great societies that did not use the wheel, but there have been no societies that did not tell stories."

–Ursula K. LeGuin, award-winning author

We've come full circle. Sales and marketing communications have gone through decades of evolution, from catchy commercial jingles to YouTube.com videos. But maybe all along we just needed to get back to our roots as humans. We began as storytellers, telling myths and parables to help understand and explain the rising sun, moon, weather, and life. "Storytelling lies at the heart of human experience—a compelling form of personal communication as ancient as language itself." [17] We're reconnecting with our humanity. We automatically listen more closely to stories than straight facts, and more readily understand and remember what we hear. Those happen to be the most critical elements in sales and marketing.

Whatever you're selling, the ability to establish trust and confidence is critical—and sets you apart from the competition. Yet those don't come easily in our skeptical society. As just a step away from a personal referral or recommendation, customer stories are unique among sales and marketing communications; no other vendor-produced communications materials carry the credibility-building impact that a success story or case study can.

---

17. *The Call of Story.* VHS. KBYU Television in association with Osric Productions, 2003.

Use the success stories within *Stories That Sell* as your inspiration, and the processes as your blueprint for a successful customer story program. If there's one thing you can do to make the process go more smoothly, it's to remain collaborative with customers throughout. Make it about them, and make them look good along the way. When produced with the customer's goals in mind, a customer story can be just as beneficial for that customer. Approach every happy customer with the objective of creating a win-win story and those projects will fall into place much more easily and be more rewarding for all.

In a broader sense, a customer story is the ultimate goal of a business relationship—the place you hope every customer reaches. When you partner with your best customers to document the positive outcome of working with your organization, then both you and the customer are acknowledging that success. It's the public declaration of the results of your partnership.

For business owners and managers so closely engaged with their products and services, it can be an emotional and gratifying experience to read one of their own customer stories. It reinforces to them that they are making a difference, and inspires them to continue making a difference.

Every day, I see storytelling bridge gaps for organizations and their customers. Companies that capture their own stories are bolstered, believing more in themselves. Potential customers find the confidence and trust they need to make purchases—taking out the leap of faith. Customer stories open doors to big accounts, expand opportunities with existing customers, help organizations land financing or grants, secure stories in major trade media, teach sales reps the value of solutions, reinforce for employees why their work matters, and support hiring.

It takes some effort and some patience. But the process itself can be quite satisfying. Out of all the things you do in your day, talking to happy customers to document successes has to be one of the more enjoyable aspects.

As you grow your business or cause, leverage the power of your most valuable sales and marketing asset—your satisfied customers—to build trust and credibility in the eyes of all your audiences. Perhaps you'll become a success story yourself of how to use customer stories. And when you do, let me know, so I can share your story with others.

Calling all Best Practices

Stories That Sell includes a number of Success-Story Marketing best practices, but perhaps you have your own best practices to share. If so, we'd love to hear them. Please email details about how you produce and use your customer stories to info@StoriesThatSellGuide.com, or go online at www.StoriesThatSellGuide.com to submit your story.

Sample Customer Stories

Following are three sample customer stories—two success stories and one case study. You can see the first two in their final layout format on pages 107-108. Look for more examples of customer stories on the book's site at www.StoriesThatSellGuide.com.

A Sample Success Story: Traditional Format

Here's a sample success story following a traditional format. (Names have been changed.)

Medical Labs Saves Almost $900,000 on Employee Benefits While Nearly Tripling in Size

[Quote to feature in the design]:

> *"We are projected to save a little under $500,000 this year on our medical, prescription, and dental benefits, as it relates to our maximum exposure...For the past three years, our total savings added up to nearly $900,000 in comparison to what the company would have spent under a traditional benefits plan."*
>
> – Michelle Matheson, Manager of Human Resources

[Callout that will run along the side in the final, designed version.]

Company:

Medical Labs

Employees:

295

Industry:

Medical

Benefit needs:
- A cost-containment strategy
- Responsive, attentive service
- Quality benefits that cover employees in every state

The Results:
- Though it has tripled in size, Medical Labs has kept benefits cost-increases well under industry averages each year, adding up to nearly $900,000 in savings to date.
- Employees are covered nationwide through the provider network.
- Almost 90 percent of employees are enrolled in benefits through Medical Labs, indicating employees have truly embraced the benefits plan.
- Benefits reports are ready in minutes.

Customer Profile

Medical Labs meets the demands of the world's most advanced medical practitioners by developing products that improve acute hospital care. Leveraging its range of clinical and commercial skills, the company develops products acquired from leading life science innovators. As a result, millions of patients undergo medical and surgical procedures more safely and comfortably each year. The company employs nearly 300 employees at its San Diego headquarters and around the country.

Employee Benefits Needs

In 2003, Medical Labs employed fewer than 100 people. Anticipating rapid growth as demand for its products increased worldwide, the company needed to evaluate new employee benefits options. At the time, its benefits were through a professional employer organization (PEO), however cost and service issues led the human resources department to seek out an alternate solution.

While many of the company's employees work at the home office, a majority of the sales reps are home-based in every state nationwide. Medical Labs wanted comprehensive coverage to suit the needs of the greatest number of employees across the country.

The Solution

Medical Labs' benefits broker introduced a self-funded plan from Self-Funded Insurance, Inc. With self-funding, Medical Labs covers actual claims incurred by employees up to a set stop-loss amount. By dramatically reducing fixed monthly premiums as compared to a fully-insured health plan, the company expected to minimize costs as it grew.

Medical Labs now offers employees one Preferred Provider Organization (PPO) plan option for medical, dental, and prescriptions, along with a flexible spending account option for all employees nationwide, regardless of location.

Today, the company has grown to about 295 employees. Almost 90 percent are enrolled in benefits through Medical Labs, indicating employees have truly embraced the Self-Funded Insurance PPO plan.

The Results

The benefits plan through Self-Funded Insurance decreases HR administration time and benefits costs for Medical Labs.

As part of her responsibilities, Matheson prepares monthly auditing reports. With reporting from Self-Funded Insurance, she can easily pull reports on employee benefits in the way she needs them – in less than two minutes. The complete auditing process, which once took a full day, now takes just a few hours.

Online tools on the Self-Funded Insurance Web site allow employees to make most of their changes on their own, rather than calling Matheson. She simply educates them about the online features. "I always direct employees to the Web site," she said. "Having claims information and the provider directory for employees to access online has meant fewer calls to the human resources department."

With the help of its broker and Self-Funded Insurance, Medical Labs has continuously adjusted its benefits to keep costs down. For example, the company previously gave employees a maximum of $2,000 for physical therapy. After that, employees paid out of pocket. For that reason, some stopped physical therapy, which resulted in additional, higher-cost claims when employees needed increased medical care for injuries. By raising the amount provided upfront for physical therapy, the company expects to reduce claims down the road.

Decisions such as that have minimized increases in benefits costs, even as the company has nearly tripled in size the past few years.

"Annual benefit renewals have been excellent," said Michelle Matheson, manager of human resources administration at Medical Labs. "Claims also look outstanding. We have had very little increase each year."

In the first year, the company saw a minimal increase, and was able to keep premiums stable for employees. The next year was just slightly higher, while the third renewal came in at about a seven percent increase. That adds up to significant savings.

"We are projected to save a little under $500,000 this year on our medical, prescription, and dental benefits," Matheson said. "What's most exciting is that we've been successful in significantly growing our employee population, while nearly doubling our plan savings from the previous year. For the past three years, our total savings added up to nearly $900,000 in comparison to what the company would have spent under a traditional benefits plan."

A Sample Success Story: Feature-Story Format

Here's a sample success story following a feature-story format. (Names have been changed.)

Winery Blends Shipping and Payment Software to Expedite Wine Orders

[Quote to feature in the design]:

> *"The time and money we save with shipping and payment automation probably add up to two full-time people. The software paid for itself the first week."*

> —Sue Sorensen, President, Oregon Winery

[Callout that will run along the side in the final, designed version.]

Company:

Oregon Winery

Industry:

Winemaking

Solution:

Shipping and payment automation solutions

Results:

- The winery runs multiple orders at once–cutting processing time from about 10 minutes down to less than 30 seconds per order.

- The ability to run multiple charges at once allowed the winery to negotiate lower transaction fees with its merchant services provider, which saves thousands annually.

- The winery prepares wine club shipments in two days instead of two weeks, and avoided having to add two full-time staff to handle the club orders.

- Savings on labor costs and credit card fees paid for the solutions the first week.

With a spirit of adventure and a passion for making world-class wine, Bob and Sue Sorensen launched Oregon Winery in the Willamette Valley in 1970. One of the first to recognize the region's value for winemaking, the winemaker has become internationally acclaimed for its Pinot Noir, Chardonnay, Pinot Gris, Pinot Blanc, Arneis, Dolcetto and White Riesling.

Today, under the second generation of leadership, the winery produces about 17,000 cases per year and is growing quickly. With direct sales–via phone, the Web site or at retail locations–expanding by 25-30 percent per year for the past few years, the company needed a more effective way to keep up with customers' specific requests and preferences, as well as help in expediting orders. The winery might send 10 shipments a day during low season, and up to 40 during high season.

Manual Shipping Becomes Unmanageable

Shipping volume reaches its highest during quarterly distribution to members of the wine club. In just a couple of years, the club has grown from 70 to 700. Previously, the winemaker struggled through a manual order fulfillment process, spending about two weeks every quarter preparing and shipping orders to club members. Each order could take more than 10 minutes of staff time to process.

"It was getting unmanageable to have just a list of customers and manual processing," said Sue Sorensen, President. "We deal with a lot of customers daily and we need to make sure we treat them more on a personal basis, remembering details like what kinds of wines they like, and ensuring that they receive their shipments on time."

Shipping & Payment Processing in One Click

When Oregon Winery selected its CRM solution, it chose to implement integrated shipping and payment processing software from XYZ Software to expedite order fulfillment. Now it's just a couple of clicks to share information across the whole system.

"There are lots of products out there that are custom-made for wine clubs or POS centers," Sorensen explained. "But we wanted a solution that would integrate with everything else we were doing—all our accounting systems, web orders, CRM and shipping. We liked XYZ Solutions because they integrate really well with our CRM software, and make it quicker to get orders out and cards charged."

Employees simply go to the customer's account record in the CRM software, and with the click of a button the order is processed end to end: the system automatically calculates the total, charges the credit card using, and triggers the shipping application to print the shipping label. The system also emails the tracking number to the customer and stores the tracking number in CRM history. All this processing is automatic once the user triggers the order processing track in the CRM system. There are no screens to click through and no cutting and pasting.

Thanks to the tight CRM integration, even off-site staff are productive. Employees who at the wine bar or at home can process orders remotely.

The Sorensens have been particularly impressed with the system's stability, finding they don't have to worry that it won't be available when it's needed most. "Shipping and payment processing work every time and are reliable, stable, easy to use and transparent. We just make sure it's on, and that's about it."

Saving Thousands on Merchant Fees, Labor Costs

With an automated process handling credit card charges and shipping preparation, the vineyard runs multiple orders at once–cutting processing time from about 10 minutes down to less than 30 seconds per order. The merchant services supported by payment processing software helped the vineyard save thousands of dollars a year on merchant fees.

Now at 700 members, and growing every day, the wine club has become much more manageable. Shipping and payment processing software tap into customers' shipping preferences and financial information in the CRM software to process orders. Sue Sorensen estimates that the winery would have had to bring on extra staff to handle the growing wine club.

"We're able to get a handle on our wine club now," she said. "Every time we do it, the list is larger. What used to take maybe two weeks, now we can do in two days."

Savings on labor costs and credit card fees drove an almost-immediate return on investment. "The time and money we save with shipping and payment automation probably add up to two full-time people," Sorensen said. "The software paid for itself the first week."

A Sample Case Study: Feature Story Format

Here's a sample case study following a feature-story format. (Names have been changed.)

Arizona IT Team Saves 100 Days a Year with Inventory Management Software

[Callout that will run along the side in the final, designed version.]

Customer

Arizona city

Industries

Government

Products

Service desk software
Inventory management software

Quick Stats

Internal customers supported: 550
IT assets: 1500
IT staff: 10

Business Benefits Realized:
- The IT director cut in half the amount of time it normally takes him to plan the next year's budget.
- The team saves 800 hours a year, or 100 workdays, with automated scanning and by giving direct access to the finance department for billing purposes.
- The city can delay hiring another staff member for a year or two, savings that pay for the software several times over.

In budget-constrained city governments, the IT department must leverage every human and physical asset to its full potential. IT directors are looking for any opportunity to extend productivity with the current staff and IT assets.

"It's a major concern making sure that we're doing as much as possible with the least amount of staff, and adding automation to delay adding more people," said Keith Hamel, IT director at an Arizona city. "Watching every penny that goes out is critical."

With about 70,000 residents and growing, the city is one of the fastest-growing communities in the Phoenix area. It's also a destination for visitors, with attractions such as arts, recreational and cultural activities.

The city employs about 550 people across nine different locations. With 10 members, the IT department keeps up with about 1500 unique IT assets. Each city department is billed quarterly for its use of certain assets, requiring IT to keep detailed records of asset allocations.

To prep for quarterly billings, IT previously had to inventory every asset manually and create spreadsheets for finance, which took a full week each quarter for the entire team. Budgeting for replacement assets likewise required more than a week since IT lacked a centralized record of that information. Manual updates were simply too taxing on the small IT department.

Agent-less Inventory Management

When considering inventory management options, the city initially explored creating a solution in house. However, the team found it too cumbersome to develop and manage its own system. With service desk software already in place to manage employees' IT issues, Hamel looked into inventory management software made by the same vendor.

The software shares a common architectural platform with the service desk solution, making it a good fit. It automatically collects and stores data in a common Configuration Management Database (CMDB), preserving data integrity and consistency throughout the asset life cycle. During employee IT calls, anyone on the team can access configuration data in the inventory software or the service desk software, allowing them to find answers more quickly.

In addition, the inventory management software also offers agent-less technology for tracking assets—a very attractive feature for Hamel.

"With other applications, you have to load the software on every machine, and then users can see the process running and possibly turn it off," he said. "Now, nothing is installed so the client sees nothing. It just grabs the information and dumps it into my database without leaving a client footprint."

As an ITIL-focused (IT Infrastructure Library) organization, the city's IT department also found the software's CMDB capabilities a draw. "This immediately gives us the ITIL foundation we need," Hamel added.

Real-Time, Automated Asset Data for Billing

The city called in the software vendor's professional services team to assist in implementation. Before coming on site, consultants evaluated the city's requirements, and then completed the implementation in just one week.

The inventory software now automatically pulls all the relevant asset information from 1,500 city technology assets, including make, model, serial number, memory, processing power, loaded software and hard drive capacity. It continuously scans the network and saves that data in the CMDB, ensuring that IT always has a current record.

The department also assigned billing codes to every asset to indicate which departments should be billed for use of a particular asset. Instead of manually assessing the inventory across nine locations, the team gives the finance department access to pull that information on its own.

"Finance needs very accurate inventory data. Now, they pull every detail they need to charge the right portion of equipment use to each department," Hamel said. "Every time they want to report on what to charge departments or determine asset depreciation for tax purposes, they get real-time information from the software."

On the help desk, agents can view the full asset inventory. It provides accurate configuration details that users may not be able to provide themselves, such as memory and processor information. In fact, Hamel finds the speed of locating asset data the most valuable benefit of the inventory management software—a capability that also supports annual budget planning.

"I'm able to very quickly determine how many machines we have of what make, model and RAM, and what software releases are on them," he said. "We know how many we need to replace in the next three years. It's no longer a guessing game."

Saving 800 Man-Hours

Detailed inventory allows the IT team to be more efficient on a day-to-day basis, as well as plan for the future in a way that maximizes use of staff and IT assets. Hamel noticed a significant difference during the last budget cycle. With a high-level view of assets, he was able to cut in half the amount of time it normally takes him to plan the next year's budget.

Plus, he's able to plan more accurately now, knowing exactly the status of all hardware and software. If the money's not in the budget for upgrades, he can more easily identify assets to move around to extend their lifespans.

Most significantly, the team cut out the quarterly preparation of billing data for the finance department. Before, five staff members spent about a week each quarter. Now, complete asset records free about 800 hours a year, or 100 workdays across the team. In this budget-conscious environment, that goes a long way toward helping IT do more without adding staff.

"As the city grows, we're able to delay hiring another staff member for another year or two," he said. "Those savings pay for the software several times over."

B

The Customer-Story Checklist

You've got a truly satisfied customer that you'd like to feature in a customer story. Ensure the process goes smoothly from start to signoff. Refer to the steps below when developing any customer story.

Strategic Story Planning (p. 27)

- Inventory your current batch of customer stories.
- Identify which stories you still need for sales, marketing, and PR needs.
- Does the proposed new story fill a current need?
- In what ways will you use the customer story?

Securing Customer Permission (p. 49)

- Arrange a call with internal stakeholders related to the customer story, such as sales reps, account managers, and marketing and/or PR team members.
- Discuss the customer's current use of products/services and the customer's perceived happiness level.
- Is now a good time to ask the customer about participating in a customer story?
- Identify key benefits for the featured customer.
- Develop the "pitch" for approaching the customer that highlights the benefits of participating.

- Determine who will ask the customer.

- During the conversation with customer contacts, ensure that all parties that will need to approve the story have given their permission before beginning.

- Consider engaging the customer's PR department as an ally in creating a customer story that benefits both sides.

- If the customer is not willing to be named in a case study or success story, decide whether an unnamed but detailed story on that organization would support your needs.

Intelligence Gathering (p. 73)

- Writers should understand the specific goals of each customer story.

- In what part of the sales cycle will it be used, and for what type of audience?

- Learn about and understand the products and services that will be featured.

- Type and save interview questions for each product and/or service on which you will create customer stories.

- Ensure interview questions are aligned with project goals.

- Gather background information from internal sources (sales and account reps) about the customer.

- Study the customer's web site and any other general information about the customer's organization.

- Tailor the general interview questionnaire with questions specific to the customer you will be interviewing to gather a unique angle.

- If there are multiple interviewees, decide whether to interview them together or separately.

- Arrange a conference line for phone interviews with multiple attendees.

- Find the best recording solution for your environment and type of phone.

Creating Compelling Stories (p. 101)

- Decide whether the story will be a case study or success story.
- Choose the format for the story (if not already established).
- Review interview notes, and prioritize the information based on project goals to find your "angle."
- Choose several relevant quotes to include.
- Write the story for the audience.
- Create an engaging opening, or "lead."
- Quantify benefits if possible.
- Create an engaging headline and subheads.
- Pull highlights into a "sidebar" so that skimmers can glean the story.
- Collect any logos, photos, or other images for the final design.

Story Signoff (p. 139)

- Circulate the customer story to internal contacts for review first.
- Determine whether you will obtain approval with a legal release form or via email.
- Email the draft of the story to the customer contact(s) with instructions for approval.
- Send the draft of the story to any resellers or partners that must be included.
- Incorporate any edits from the customer.
- Remain politely persistent as you work toward final signoff.
- Bring in key internal and customer contacts if you run into any approval roadblocks.
- Formally thank customers.

Index

S

About the Author

Casey Hibbard, founder and president of Compelling Cases, Inc. (www.compelling-cases.com), has helped dozens of companies create more than 450 customer stories over the past decade. She has produced and managed success stories and case studies for companies such as Macrovision, Jobfox, USA.NET, IHS, and Vocus. Casey is featured in numerous books, articles, and teleclasses on the topic. She consults with organizations one-on-one and conducts online customer-story classes.

Keep up with conversation and best practices related to customer stories with the free *Stories That Sell* e-Tip of the Month and the *Stories That Sell* Blog. Both are available at www.StoriesThatSellGuide.com.